ST. KITTS AND NEVIS TRAVEL GUIDE 2023-2024

The Ultimate Guide to Exploring the Islands Top Attractions and Activities, Itinerary, where to stay, Culture and History of St. Kitts and Nevis

GENEVA WALKER

Table of Contents

INTRODUCTION

My amazing experience to St. Kitts and Nevis

I have always been intrigued by the Caribbean islands, with their rich culture, history, and stunning natural beauty. When I finally got the chance to visit St. Kitts and Nevis, I was thrilled and eager to explore these two amazing West Indies destinations. Here is a rundown of how I planned and savored my trip to these incredible places.

Planning my vacation

I made the decision to visit St. Kitts and Nevis between December and April, the dry season, when the weather was bright and pleasant and had little chance of a storm. I scheduled my trip to Basseterre, the capital of St. Kitts, with a layover in Miami. The flight took roughly 16 hours in total, but it was worth it.

I also booked my accommodation in advance, picking a nice and reasonable guesthouse in Basseterre for the first four nights and a gorgeous seaside cottage in Nevis for the remaining three nights. I wanted to experience both islands and their diverse atmosphere.

I researched the sites and activities I wanted to do on each island, using this travel book as a reference. I produced a list of things I wanted to see, such as the Brimstone Hill Fortress, the Romney Manor, the picturesque railway, the Nevis Peak, and the waterfalls. I also looked for adventure and sports choices, such as diving, snorkeling, golfing, and ziplining.

I opted to rent a car for the first four days in St. Kitts to tour the island at my leisure and convenience. I also booked a ferry ticket from St. Kitts to Nevis on the fifth day of my trip. I planned to use public transportation or taxis on Nevis, as the island is smaller and easier to move around.

Enjoying my trip

I landed in Basseterre on a lovely morning in January 2023. I was greeted by the pleasant employees at the airport, who helped me with my bags and immigration processes. I took a taxi to my guesthouse, where I checked in and rested for a while.

I spent the first day touring Basseterre, meandering along its colorful streets and enjoying its colonial architecture. I toured Independence Square, the Berkeley Memorial Clock Tower, the National Museum, and the Cathedral of Immaculate Conception. I also had local specialties at a nearby eatery, such as goat water stew, saltfish cakes, and coconut bread.

The next day, I traveled to the Brimstone Hill Fortress, a UNESCO World Heritage Site formerly a British bastion against the French. I was awed by the spectacular defenses and guns overlooking the Caribbean Sea. I learned about the history of the stronghold and its part in the fights between the European powers.

I next traveled to the Romney Manor, a historic sugar plantation that is now home to the Caribelle Batik, a local handicraft shop that manufactures gorgeous fabrics employing wax-resist dying processes. I witnessed a demonstration of how the batik is manufactured and bought some souvenirs for my family and friends.

On the third day, I did the scenic railway excursion, a fascinating way to explore the island from a different perspective. The train rides along a historic sugar cane railway track that revolves around St. Kitts. It offers spectacular views of the mountains, valleys, villages, and coasts. The tour also includes narrative, music, snacks, and drinks.

On the fourth day, I traveled to the Mount Liamuiga volcano, the highest point in St. Kitts at 1,156 meters above sea level. I joined a guided hike to the crater rim, which took about four hours round trip. The hike was tough but rewarding, as I observed some magnificent flora and fauna along the way, such as monkeys, hummingbirds, orchids, and ferns. The view from the summit was breathtaking.

On the fifth day, I checked out from my guesthouse and took a ferry to Nevis, only around three kilometers from St. Kitts. The ferry voyage was calm and gorgeous, and it took about 45 minutes to reach Charlestown, the city of Nevis. I took a taxi to my cottage, where I checked in and rested on the beach.

I spent the sixth day going to the Nevis Peak, which is another volcanic mountain that rises 985 meters above sea level. The hike was more difficult than Mount Liamuiga, as it involved some steep slopes and slick rocks. However, the panorama was equally spectacular, and I felt a sense of accomplishment when I reached the summit.

I spent the seventh day diving and snorkeling in the pristine waters of Nevis. I joined a local diving business that took me to some of the top locations surrounding the island, such as the Booby High Shoals, the Monkey Shoals, and the Coconut Tree Reef. I witnessed magnificent aquatic life, such as turtles, rays, sharks, and colorful fish. I also played golf at the Four Seasons Resort, a lovely 18-hole course that views the sea and the mountains.

I departed from Nevis on the ninth day and flew back to Miami. I had a fantastic trip to St. Kitts & Nevis and would want to return sometime.

This travel guide will help you enjoy and have a fantastic time on your trip/vacation to St. Kitts and Nevis because it will:

- Introduce you to the islands' rich and varied culture so that you may learn about colonial history, regional customs, music, festivals, food, and other things like arts, crafts, and architecture.

- Show you the natural beauty and animals of the islands, where you may explore the volcanic mountains, the rainforest, the beaches, and the coral reefs and see the monkeys, hummingbirds, orchids, and ferns.

- Suggest the best sights and activities that suit your interests and preferences, whether you seek history, nature, adventure, or sports.

- Guide you on planning your itinerary, choosing your lodging and dining alternatives, moving around the islands, and dealing with immigration, customs, currency, language, climate, emergency, and health issues.

Why visit St. Kitts and Nevis?

Two small Caribbean islands, St. Kitts and Nevis, provide a special fusion of scenic beauty, cultural variety, and charming history. Whether searching for a relaxed beach holiday, an adventurous outdoor adventure, or a rich cultural experience, you will find something to fit your taste in St. Kitts and Nevis.

Here are some of the reasons why you should visit St. Kitts and Nevis in 2023 or 2024:

Explore the gorgeous scenery: St. Kitts and Nevis are blessed with lush green mountains, volcanic peaks, rainforests, waterfalls, and coral reefs. You may trek to the crater lake of Mount Liamuiga, the highest point of St. Kitts, or take a picturesque railway tour across the island. You may also snorkel or dive in the beautiful waters of The Narrows, the waterway that separates the two islands, or enjoy the views from the golden beaches of Pinney's Beach on Nevis.

Experience the unique culture: St. Kitts and Nevis have a rich and varied cultural heritage influenced by African, European, and Caribbean traditions. At the UNESCO World

Heritage Site of Brimstone Hill Fortress on St. Kitts, you may study about the history of slavery, sugar plantations, and colonial warfare. Alternatively, you can go to the Museum of Nevis History to find out where Alexander Hamilton, known as one of the founding fathers of the United states was born. Additionally, you may sample the regional cuisine, which includes goat water, a hot stew; stewed saltfish, the meal's national dish; and sugar cake, a sweet coconut treat. You may also experience the local cuisine, which offers goat water, a fiery stew; stewed saltfish, the national dish; and sugar cake, a sweet coconut delicacy.

Enjoy the festive atmosphere: St. Kitts and Nevis are recognized for their brilliant and colorful festivals, which showcase their music, dance, and art. You can join the Carnival on St. Kitts from mid-December to early January, where you can witness parades, pageants, and masquerades, or attend the Culturama on Nevis from late July to early August, where you can enjoy calypso competitions, street jams, and cultural events. You can also catch other events throughout the year, such as the St. Kitts Music Festival in June or the Nevis Blues Festival in April.

St. Kitts and Nevis are islands that fascinate you with their natural wonders, cultural richness, and festive atmosphere. They are wonderful destinations for those who want to experience the Caribbean differently. This travel guide will assit you in planning your trip to St. Kitts and Nevis in 2023-2024, with recommendations on where to stay, what to do, and how to get around. You will also find important information about visa requirements, health and safety measures, and local cultures. With this travel guide, you will be set to tour St. Kitts and Nevis and have a great trip.

How to get there and around

The Caribbean Sea is home to the islands of St. Kitts and Nevis, which are divided by The Narrows, a narrow passageway. They form a sovereign nation member of the Commonwealth of Nations. The islands are famed for their natural beauty, rich history, and vibrant culture.

By plane

The primary airport in St. Kitts and Nevis is Robert L. Bradshaw International Airport (SKB), located on the northeast coast of St. Kitts, near the capital city of Basseterre. The airport has direct flights to and from major cities in North America, Europe, and the Caribbean, including New York, London, Toronto, Miami, Antigua, and San Juan. Some airlines that serve SKB are American Airlines, British Airways, Air Canada, Delta Air Lines, United Airlines, and Seaborne.

The smaller Vance W. Amory International Airport (NEV) is located on the north coast of Nevis, near Charlestown. The airport has regional flights to and from Antigua, St. Maarten, St. Thomas, and Tortola, operated by airlines such as LIAT, Winair, Tradewind Aviation, and Cape Air.

To get between the two islands by air, you can take a short journey with either FlyMontserrat or Trans Anguilla Airways. The flight time is roughly 10 minutes, and the fee is around US$100 one way.

By boat

Another alternative to get between St. Kitts and Nevis is via boat. Many ferry routes operate daily between Basseterre and Charlestown, as well as between Majors Bay on the southeast point of St. Kitts and Oualie Beach on the northwest coast of Nevis. The ferry voyage takes around 45 minutes and costs around US$10 one way.

You can also take a water taxi or a private charter boat to explore the islands at your own pace. Various operators offer these services, such as Blue Water Safaris, Leeward Islands Charters, Funky Monkey Tours, and Nevis Yacht Charters. You should pay roughly US $ 150 to US $ 200 per hour for a water taxi or a charter boat.

By road

The best way to move around St. Kitts and Nevis by road is by renting a car or a scooter. You can locate various rental firms at the airports or main cities, such as Avis, Thrifty, TDC Car Rental, Hertz, and Nevis Auto Rental. To hire a car, you will need both an international driving permit and a current driver's license from your home country. You must also obtain a temporary local driver's license for US$25 at the rental business or the police station.

Driving is done on the left side of the road in St. Kitts and Nevis. The roads are generally well-maintained but narrow and twisting, especially in mountainous areas. Be aware of potholes, speed bumps, pedestrians, animals, and other cars on the road. On roads, the speed limit is 80 km/h (50 mph), but in urban areas it is 40 km/h (25 mph).

If you choose not to drive yourself, you can alternatively use a cab or a bus to move about the islands. Taxis are plentiful and easy to obtain at airports, hotels, ferry terminals, and tourist destinations. They are metered, but you can also arrange a set fare before you start your journey. A typical taxi ticket from SKB to Basseterre is roughly US$12, and from NEV to Charlestown is around $8.

Buses are cheaper but less reliable than cabs. They are minibusses or vans that run along defined routes between the principal towns and villages on both islands. They have green license plates with the letter H or HA on them. You can flag down a bus anywhere along the road or wait at a bus stop. The fee is normally between US$1 and US$3, depending on the distance.

When to go and what to pack

St. Kitts and Nevis are year-round attractions, offering warm and sunny weather, lovely beaches, and lush wildlife. However, certain months may be more ideal than others depending on your preferences and budget. Here are some elements to consider when organizing your trip:

Climate

The average temperature of St. Kitts and Nevis varies from 25.5 °C (78 °F) in January and February to 28 °C (82 °F) between June and October. The trade winds, which blow more regularly from January to April and hence are colder and drier than the rest of the year, makes the island chill. The rainy season extends from July through November, when showers and thunderstorms are more frequent and intense, particularly on the higher slopes. The islands are also vulnerable to hurricanes during this period, but the biggest storms frequently spare them.

High and low season

From mid-December to mid-April, when the weather is dry and lovely, is considered St. Kitts and Nevis' peak season, and the islands attract numerous visitors from North

America and Europe. This is also the peak time for festivals and events, such as the St. Kitts Music Festival in June, the Nevis Culturama in July-August, and the St. Kitts-Nevis National Carnival in December-January. The negative of this season is that prices for flights, hotels, and activities are higher, and availability is limited. You may need to reserve far in advance to secure your position.

The low season extends from mid-April to mid-December, when the weather is hotter and wetter, and the islands are less crowded. This is a terrific time to enjoy lower rates and more flexibility and experience the islands at a slower pace. You may also find some bargains and discounts during this period. However, you should also be prepared for certain closures and decreased services, especially in September and October, when some hotels and restaurants close for repair or vacation.

What to pack

Regardless of when you visit St. Kitts and Nevis, you should pack lightweight, comfortable clothing that can shield you from the rain and sun.

Here are some basic goods that you should bring:

- Passport, visa (if required), travel insurance paperwork, health insurance card, copies of claim forms, and any other important documents.

- a current driver's license or an international driving license if you want to hire a vehicle (if your license is not in English).

- A credit or debit card that works globally (ideally with a chip) or enough cash in US dollars or Eastern Caribbean dollars (the local currency).

- A smartphone or tablet with charger that can access the internet, make calls, send messages, take pictures, and use applications, as well as one that has a local SIM card (or an international roaming plan).

- A power adapter that can fit the local sockets (type A or B) or a universal adapter that can function in any country.

- A bag or suitcase that can fit your items and meet the airline's weight and size constraints.

- A daypack or tote bag that can carry your essentials while you go out.

- A water bottle that can be refilled with filtered or purified water (or water purification pills if you like).

- A sunscreen (SPF 15 or higher) with UVA and UVB protection, sunglasses, a hat, and lip balm to protect yourself from sun exposure.

- An insect repellent containing DEET, picaridin, IR3535, lemon eucalyptus (OLE) oil, para-menthane-diol (PMD), or 2-undecanone to prevent bug bites.

- A first-aid kit that contains bandages, gauze, adhesive tape, antiseptic wound cleanser, antibacterial ointment, hydrocortisone cream, antihistamine, pain reliever, anti-diarrhea medicine, motion sickness medicine, oral rehydration salts, thermometer, scissors, tweezers, eye drops, disposable gloves, etc.

- A personal hygiene kit that contains a toothbrush, toothpaste, dental floss, shampoo, conditioner, soap, deodorant, razor, shaving cream, comb, brush, nail clipper, nail file, tampons/pads/cups, etc.

- A personal safety kit contains condoms, earplugs, flashlights, whistles, etc.

- A swimsuit, beach towel, flip-flops, water shoes, snorkel gear (or rent it on the island), and a waterproof bag or case for your valuables.

- A lightweight jacket, cardigan, or sweater that can keep you warm at night or in air-conditioned locations.

- A rain jacket, umbrella, or poncho that can keep you dry in case of showers or storms.

- A casual attire that can be worn for touring, dinner, or nightlife. This may be a polo shirt, khaki pants, and loafers for men. This could be a dress, skirt, or slacks with a shirt and sandals for ladies.

- Formal clothing can be worn for important occasions like weddings, ceremonies, or upscale restaurants. This could be a suit, shirt, tie, and dress shoes for men. This may be a cocktail dress, heels, and jewelry for women.

- A hiking costume can be used for outdoor activities like hiking, biking, ziplining, or golfing. This may be a T-shirt, shorts, sneakers, socks, and a cap for men and women.

- A laundry bag or kit that can let you wash and dry your garments if needed.

To conclude, when to go and what to bring for your trip to St. Kitts and Nevis depends on your particular preferences and budget. However, you can use this chapter as a guide to help you make the best option. You can also check the latest weather forecasts, travel advisories, and COVID-19 protocols before you schedule your trip. St. Kitts and Nevis are lovely islands that provide something for everyone, whether you are searching for history, culture, nature, adventure, or relaxation.

Travel tips and safety guidance

The Caribbean twin-island nation of St. Kitts and Nevis welcomes tourists with a wide range of attractions. Whether you want to explore the rich history and culture, appreciate the natural beauty and animals, or relax on the pristine beaches and indulge in the local cuisine, St. Kitts and Nevis has something for everyone. However, before you start your vacation, here are some travel tips and safety information to help you get the most out of your trip.

Travel tips

Transportation: The easiest method to move around St. Kitts and Nevis is by taxi, which is plentiful and economical. You may also hire a vehicle, but you'll need to pay EC$62.50 to the police station or the car rental company for a temporary license. You need to drive on the left side of the road and be aware of small lanes, potholes, and pedestrians. Another option is to take public buses, which are cheap and frequent but may not follow a defined timetable or itinerary. You can also embark on a ferry or a water taxi between the two islands.

Climate and clothing: The year-round highs of St. Kitts and Nevis range from 23°C to 31°C due to its tropical environment. From May through November, Occasionally, hurricanes and tropical storms may occur during the rainy season. The dry season, which has colder nights and lower humidity, lasts from December to April. You should take light apparel, such as cotton shirts, shorts, skirts, and sandals. You should pack a hat, sunglasses, sunscreen, insect repellent, and a raincoat or umbrella. If you plan to visit religious places or fancy restaurants, you may need to dress more conservatively or formally.

Safety advice

Crime: St. Kitts and Nevis is typically safe for tourists, but there have been incidences of crime, such as armed robbery and assault. You should use caution and avoid walking alone at night, especially in secluded locations or unknown communities. You should also secure your valuables safely or leave them at home. If you are a victim of a crime, report it to the police immediately.

Health: St. Kitts and Nevis have adequate health facilities for basic medical care, although major situations may necessitate evacuation to another country.You should have adequate travel insurance that includes repatriation and medical costs. You should also contact your doctor at least a month before your trip to acquire any necessary vaccines or medicines. Some recommended immunizations are hepatitis A, typhoid, tetanus, diphtheria, and measles. You should also avoid drinking tap water or eating raw or undercooked food to prevent diarrhea or other diseases.

Natural disasters: Natural catastrophes including hurricanes, earthquakes, volcanic eruptions, landslides, and floods are common in St. Kitts and Nevis. You should check the weather forecasts and follow the advice of local authorities in case of an emergency. You should also have an emergency kit with basics such as water, food, flashlight, radio, phone charger, first aid kit, and copies of your documentation.

For visitors, tourist of all ages and interests, St. Kitts and Nevis is a fantastic location that provides a combination of culture, nature, and entertainment. Following these travel guidelines and safety guidance may guarantee that your vacation is pleasurable and hassle-free. This guide to St.

Kitts and Nevis 2023-2024 will aid you with having a fascinating journey to this Caribbean paradise.

CHAPTER 1

History and Culture

St. Kitts and Nevis known as the twin-island republic in the Caribbean has a rich history and culture. The ancient Carib people first inhabited the islands, who named them Liamuiga (fertile island) and Oualie (land of beautiful seas). Later, the French and the British conquered the islands, using enslaved Africans to labor on the sugar plantations. The islands witnessed several battles and conflicts between the colonial powers, as well as rebellions and resistance activities by the enslaved Africans. Since their 1983 separation from Britain, the islands have developed own identities and organizations.

In this travel guidebook, we will expose you to the history and culture of St. Kitts and Nevis and give you some ideas and recommendations on how to appreciate its history and culture.

Some of the places that we will cover in this book are:

- The colonial past and the road to freedom

- The people and their traditions
- The music, festivals, and gastronomy
- The arts, crafts, and architecture
- These are only some of the goodies that await you in this chapter.

The colonial past and the road to freedom

St. Kitts and Nevis have a long and stormy history of colonization, resistance, and emancipation, which has impacted their identity, culture, and politics. The islands were among the first in the Caribbean inhabited by Europeans. Still, they also experienced the battles of the indigenous people, the enslaved Africans, and the free blacks against oppression and exploitation. Here are some of the important events and individuals that distinguished their colonial past and their route to independence:

The first colonies

St. Kitts was spotted by Christopher Columbus in 1493, who named it San Cristóbal after his patron saint. Because of the cloud cover on its top, he also gave Nevis the name Nuestra Seora de las Nieves which means Our Lady of the Snows). However, he did not land on either island, inhabited by the Carib people, who rejected the Spanish attempts to colonize them.

Sir Thomas Warner led the English in founding the first long-term European colony on St. Kitts in 1623. He came with 15 settlers and formed a partnership with the Carib leader Ouboutou Tegremante. The next year, a French expedition led by Pierre Belain d'Esnambuc landed on the island and joined forces with the English against the Spanish. The two nations agreed to partition St. Kitts, with the English occupying the central half and the French occupying the northern and southern parts.

Nevis was founded by the English in 1628 under Anthony Hilton, who had relocated from St. Kitts with 80 inhabitants. Nevis swiftly became one of the most successful colonies in the Caribbean, producing sugar, tobacco, cotton, indigo, and ginger. It also became a shelter for Puritans, Quakers, Jews, and other religious dissenters who fled persecution in England.

The sugar revolution

The 1640s saw the beginning of sugar cane farming, which had major impact on St. Kitts and Nevis' economy and social structure. Sugar became the principal export product and source of riches for the planters, who purchased enormous estates and imported thousands of enslaved Africans to labor on them. The sugar business also spurred the growth of trade, infrastructure, and urbanization on the islands.

However, sugar also produced social difficulties and disputes. The enslaved Africans experienced severe conditions and brutal treatment on the estates and often rebelled against their enslavers. The most noteworthy insurrection happened in 1639 on St. Kitts, when roughly 300 Africans captured a fort and held it for several weeks until a combined army of English and French troops crushed them.

The planters also faced external dangers from other European countries, especially France and Spain, who periodically attacked and raided their possessions. The most destructive raid came in 1706 when a French fleet led by François de Troyes conquered St. Kitts and destroyed most of its plantations and structures. The British regained the island in 1713 via the Treaty of Utrecht, The colonial past, and the road to independence.

The abolition of slavery and the rise of the free blacks

A major turning event in the history of St. Kitts and Nevis was the abolition of slavery throughout the British Empire in 1834. The enslaved Africans were freed, but they had to serve a period of apprenticeship until 1838 when they became emancipated. The emancipated Africans experienced many hurdles and sufferings, including poverty, discrimination, and lack of land and education. However, they also showed tenacity and inventiveness, building their villages, churches, schools, and organizations.

One of the most outstanding examples of free black achievement was constructing the first self-governing town in the Caribbean on Nevis in 1840. The town was called New River or Gingerland, and it was created by James Stephen Weekes, a formerly enslaved person who became a wealthy businessman and landowner. He bought a big estate from his previous master and split it among his fellow freedmen, who elected him as their mayor. The town had its own council, court, police, school, and church, and it prospered until the late 19th century.

Another noteworthy figure of the free black movement was Thomas Berkeley Hardtman Berkeley, who was born in St.

Kitts in 1854 to a former slave mother and a white father. He became a lawyer, politician, and journalist, advocating for the rights and interests of the black majority. He created the St. Kitts-Nevis-Anguilla Labour Party in 1932, the first political party in the Caribbean. He also spearheaded the workers' protests against the low salaries and bad conditions on the sugar farms in 1935-36, which resulted in some reforms and concessions from the colonial authorities.

The Federation and the independence

St. Kitts and Nevis became members of the Federation of the West Indies in 1958, which was an attempt to construct a political union among the British Caribbean territories. However, the federation soon disintegrated in 1962 due to internal rivalries and disagreements. St. Kitts and Nevis then merged with Anguilla to become a separate colony within the British Commonwealth in 1967, with a degree of autonomy and self-government.

However, Anguilla quickly rebelled against the union and declared its independence in 1969, which led to a brief intervention by British forces. Anguilla eventually split from

St. Kitts and Nevis in 1980, becoming a British overseas colony.

St. Kitts and Nevis resumed their pursuit for full independence under the leadership of Robert Llewellyn Bradshaw, who became the island's first Premier in 1967. He was followed by his deputy Paul Southwell in 1978, who died shortly after taking office. The next Premier was Lee Moore, who oversaw the negotiations with Britain for independence.

St. Kitts and Nevis ultimately gained independence on September 19, 1983, becoming a sovereign state within the Commonwealth of Nations. Kennedy Simmonds, the leader of the People's Action Movement (PAM), which had opposed Bradshaw's Labour Party (SKNLP), was the country's first prime minister. The islands chose a constitutional monarchy with a parliamentary democracy, with Queen Elizabeth II serving as the head of state.

Since then, St. Kitts and Nevis have had political and economic issues since then. However, they have also made some developments and achievements, such as diversifying their economy, growing their tourism industry, reducing their poverty rate, upgrading their education system, and boosting their regional integration.

The people and their traditions

St. Kitts and Nevis are home to a warm and welcoming people with a rich and diverse cultural past. The islands' population is predominantly of African heritage but also includes evidence of European, Carib, and Indian influences. The people of St. Kitts and Nevis are proud of their history, traditions, and identity, and they express them via their music, dance, art, cuisine, and festivals.

Here are some of the characteristics of the islands' culture that you can explore in 2023-2024:

Music: Music is a vital element of the island's culture, and it reflects the blending of African rhythms, European melodies, and Caribbean influences. The most popular genres include calypso, soca, reggae, and steelpan, played at numerous festivals and places throughout the year. Some local musical icons are King Starshield, a legendary calypso singer; Ellie Matt, a renowned soca artist; and the Small Axe Band, a notable reggae group.

Dance: Dance is another method of commemorating the islands' culture, highlighting the performers' ingenuity and skill. Some of the traditional dances are masquerade, a colorful and vibrant dance that combines masks, costumes, and acrobatic moves; moko-jumbies, a spectacular dance that features stilt-walkers; and clowns, a hilarious dance that mocks the colonial masters. Some of the modern dances are salsa, bachata, and zouk, which are influenced by Latin American forms.

Art: Art is another way of expression on the islands, extending from paintings, sculptures, pottery, and batik to jewelry. Some of the local artists are Kate Spencer, a painter who captures the beauty of nature; Roosevelt Taylor, a sculptor who uses driftwood and metal; Monica Huggins, a potter who creates functional and decorative pieces; Caribelle Batik, a company that produces vibrant fabrics; and ZIZI Jewellery, a brand that offers unique accessories.

St. Kitts and Nevis are home to a warm and welcoming people with a rich and diverse cultural past. The islands' population is predominantly of African heritage but also includes evidence of European, Carib, and Indian influences. The people of St. Kitts and Nevis are proud of their history, traditions, and identity, and they express them via their music, dance, art, cuisine, and festivals.

Music, festivals, and gastronomy

A rich and varied cultural legacy influenced by African, European, and Caribbean customs is shared by the islands of St. Kitts and Nevis. The islands are recognized for their lively music, colorful festivals, and wonderful cuisine, which reflect their history, identity, and personality.

Music

Music is a vital aspect of life in St. Kitts and Nevis; you can hear it everywhere, from the streets to the churches to the nightclubs. The islands have produced numerous outstanding musicians who have left their impact on the regional and worldwide stage, such as Kim Collins, Masud Sadiki, Nicha B, Infamus, and Dejour.

The most popular genres of music in St. Kitts and Nevis are calypso, soca, reggae, dancehall, and gospel. Calypso is a kind of music that has its roots in Trinidad and Tobago and is distinguished by its humorous lyrics that make political and social commentary. Soca is a mix of calypso and soul music that is lively and vibrant. Reggae is a Jamaican form of music influenced by ska, rocksteady, and R&B. Dancehall is a type of reggae that is quicker and more rhythmic. Gospel music is a genre of Christian music that draws inspiration from soul, blues, and jazz.

One of the greatest ways to enjoy the music of St. Kitts and Nevis is to attend the annual St. Kitts Music Festival[https://www.stkittstourism.kn/music-festival], which is held in late June at the Warner Park Stadium in Basseterre. The festival comprises local and international performers who play a variety of genres, such as Burna Boy, Koffee, Gramps Morgan, Wizkid, Kes The Band, Chronixx, Machel Montano, and more. The event also features island-wide festivities, including beach parties, boat cruises, after-parties, and midday music.

Another musical event you may enjoy in St. Kitts and Nevis is the Nevis Blues Festival, held in early April at the Oualie Beach Resort in Nevis. The festival showcases local and worldwide blues performers who play on a beachfront stage under the stars. The event also includes workshops, jam sessions, and cultural trips.

Festivals

Festivals are another way to celebrate the culture of St. Kitts and Nevis, and there are several to select from throughout the year. The most major event is the National Carnival, which is annually from mid-December to early January in both islands. The carnival features parades, competitions, shows, parties, and masquerades that showcase the creativity and talent of the people. The centerpieces of the carnival include the Sugar Mas Parade, which is a procession of colorful costumes and floats on New Year's Day in St. Kitts, and the Culturama Parade, which is a similar celebration on Emancipation Day (August 1) in Nevis.

Other festivals that you can enjoy in St. Kitts and Nevis are the St. Kitts Food Festival, which is held in late October and showcases the culinary diversity of the island; the Nevis Mango Festival, which is held in early July and celebrates the delicious fruit with cooking demonstrations, competitions, tastings, and live music; the St. Kitts Chocolate Festival, which is held in late May and features chocolate-themed events such as workshops, tours, dinners, and spa treatments; and the Nevis Kite Flying Festival, which is held on Easter Monday (April 17) and attracts kite enthusiasts from all over the world.

Cuisine

Cuisine is another facet of culture that you may savor in St. Kitts and Nevis. The islands have a diverse culinary legacy that incorporates African, European, Indian, and Caribbean influences. The basic foods are rice, beans, breadfruit, yams, cassava, and plantains, which are commonly cooked with coconut milk, spices, and herbs. The main protein sources include fish, chicken, goat, hog, and beef, frequently grilled, roasted, stewed, or curried. Some of the usual dishes that you can try in St. Kitts and Nevis are:

1. **Pelau:** A one-pot dish of rice cooked with chicken or pork, pigeon peas, coconut milk, and vegetables.

2. **Goat water:** A substantial stew containing goat meat, breadfruit, green papaya, dumplings, and spices.

3. Saltfish: A meal of salted cod fish cooked with tomatoes, onions, peppers, and herbs.

4. Johnny cakes: Fried bread from flour, water, baking powder, and salt.

5. **Conch:** A sort of marine snail that is prepared in many ways, such as soup, salad, cakes, or curry.

6. **Roti:** A flatbread of Indian origin filled with meat or vegetable curries.

7. **Souse:** A dish of boiled pig's feet or chicken feet seasoned with lime juice, onions, cucumbers, and chili peppers.

8. **Black pudding:** A type of sausage made from pig's blood, rice, spices, and herbs.

To accompany your dinner, you can sip some of the local beverages, such as:

1. **Ting:** A pleasant soda prepared from grapefruit juice and carbonated water.

2. **Carib:** A popular lager beer manufactured in St. Kitts and Nevis.

3. **Rum punch:** A cocktail containing rum, lime juice, grenadine, and bitters.

4. **Mauby:** A bitter-sweet drink produced from the bark of the mauby tree, sugar, and spices.

5. **Sorrel:** A festive cocktail made from the dried petals of the sorrel plant, sugar, ginger, and rum.

For dessert, you can indulge in some of the local delights, such as:

1. **Coconut bread:** A moist and dense bread made using grated coconut, flour, sugar, eggs, and spices.

2. **Tamarind balls:** A sweet prepared with tamarind pulp, sugar, and spices shaped into balls and covered with sugar.

3. **Guava cheese:** A fudge-like dessert from guava pulp, sugar, and lime juice.

4. **Sugar cake:** A chewy sweet made with grated coconut, sugar, and food coloring.

St. Kitts and Nevis is a treasure mine of creative and cultural expressions representing the islands' rich and diverse heritage. From the colonial fortifications to the contemporary galleries, from the traditional crafts to the innovative designs, you will sure find plenty of opportunities to observe and appreciate the ingenuity and ability of the local artists and artisans.

Arts and Crafts

St. Kitts and Nevis boasts a flourishing arts and crafts culture that exhibits the ability and inventiveness of the islanders. Various handmade products employ natural materials such as wood, clay, stone, coral, shells, seeds, and fibers. Some of the most popular goods are pottery, baskets, jewelry, paintings, sculptures, carvings, masks, dolls, and batik textiles.

You can browse and buy these unusual items at numerous shops, marketplaces, and studios around the islands. Some of the best sites to visit are:

Rogers' Souvenir & Crafts: This is a modest craft boutique in Basseterre that carries a limitless variety of local and regional handicrafts. You may get everything from postcards and magnets to paintings and sculptures. The shop is open from Monday to Saturday from 9:00 a.m. to 5:00 p.m. The pricing is moderate and negotiable. The closest hotel is Ocean Terrace Inn, which is a 4-star hotel featuring a pool, a restaurant, and a bar. The average price per night is $150.

Nevis Craft House: This is a cooperative of local artisans who manufacture high-quality crafts utilizing traditional techniques and materials. You can find pottery, baskets, quilts, dolls, and more. The craft house is located in Charlestown along the sea. The opening time starts from 8:30 a.m. to 4:30 p.m, which runs from monday to Friday. The costs are reasonable and fixed. The Hamilton Beach Villas & Spa is the closest hotel, a 4-star hotel featuring a beachfront position, spa, and restaurant. The average price per night is $250.

Vaughn Anslyn Design: This is a studio and gallery of Vaughn Anslyn, a prominent artist specializing in portraiture, murals, event décor, signage, woodwork, and body painting. You can enjoy his vivid and passionate artwork or commission your own. The studio is located in Frigate Bay near the golf course. It is open by appointment only. The cost varies depending on how big and complicated the assignment is. The closest hotel is St. Kitts Marriott Resort & The Royal Beach Casino, a 5-star hotel with a casino, a golf course, and a spa. The average price per night is $300.

Charlestown Gallery: This premier art gallery in Nevis showcases works by local and international artists. You can see paintings, sculptures, prints, photography, and more. The gallery is located in Charlestown near the Hamilton House Museum. It is open from Monday to Saturday from 10:00 a.m. to 5:00 p.m. The pricing is moderate and negotiable. The closest hotel is Montpelier Plantation & Beach, a 5-star hotel featuring a historic plantation home, a pool, and a private beach. The average price per night is $400.

Architecture

St. Kitts and Nevis has a rich architectural heritage that stretches from the 17th to the 21st century. The islands have undergone various changes in styles and influences over the years, from the European colonial powers to the enslaved Africans to the current developers. You can view examples of military, religious, civic, residential, and commercial architecture that reflect the history and culture of the islands.

Some of the most prominent architectural landmarks are:

Brimstone Hill Fortress National Park: This is an extraordinary example of 17th- and 18th-century military architecture in a Caribbean context. It is a UNESCO World Heritage Site that was conceived by the British and erected by African slave labor. It comprises many structures on different heights of a steep volcanic slope that offer beautiful views of the sea and the surrounding islands. The park is open every day from 9:30 a.m. until 5:30 p.m. The entrance price is $15 for adults and $7 for children.

St. George's Anglican Church: This is one of the oldest churches in St. Kitts that dates back to 1670. It is a Gothic Revival-style tower with a stone façade, stained glass windows, wooden pews, and a pipe organ. It is located in Basseterre near Independence Square. The church is open every day from 8:00 a.m. until 4:00 p.m. There is no entrance cost. However, donations are encouraged.

Romney Manor: This is a former sugar plantation that dates back to the 17th century. It is now home to Caribelle Batik, a notable batik fabric company that uses old wax-resist dying techniques. You can view demonstrations of batik making or shop for apparel and accessories. You can also visit the lovely gardens that include exotic plants and trees. The manor is open every day from 9:00 a.m. to 5:00 p.m. The entrance cost is $3 for adults and $1 for youngsters.

Montpelier mansion: This is a former plantation mansion that dates back to the 18th century. It is currently a premium hotel that offers elegant lodging and fine dining. It is also a historic spot where Lord Nelson married Fanny Nisbet in 1787. You may see the actual marriage certificate and other souvenirs in the museum. The house is open every day from 8:00 a.m. until 10:00 p.m. The entrance cost to the museum is $5 for adults and $2 for youngsters.

The Hermitage Plantation Inn: The oldest wooden house in the Caribbean dates back to the 17th century. It is a delightful hotel with pleasant rooms and cottages, a restaurant, a bar, and a pool. You can also enjoy horseback riding, hiking, and yoga. The inn is open everyday from 7:00 a.m. until 11:00 p.m. The entrance cost to the residence is $10 for adults and $5 for youngsters.

The Hamilton House: Alexander Hamilton, one of the founding fathers of the United States, was born in this renovated Georgian-style home. It is currently a museum that shows exhibits and artifacts linked to his life and legacy. It is located in Charlestown near the waterfront. The museum is open from Monday to Friday from 9:00 a.m. to 4:00 p.m. The entry price is $10 for adults and $5 for children.

Conclusion

The arts, crafts, and architecture of St. Kitts and Nevis reflect the islands' rich and diverse heritage. They display the ingenuity and talent of the indigenous artists and craftspeople, as well as the history and culture of the islands. Whether you seek unusual souvenirs, gorgeous views, or historic places, you will find many options to fit your taste and budget. You can visit various stores, marketplaces, studios, galleries, museums, parks, churches, plantations, and hotels that offer a variety of products and services. You can also learn more about the tales and individuals behind these artistic and architectural landmarks. You will be in awe of the islands' beauty and variety as well as its art, culture, and history. This chapter has presented you with some of the top destinations to visit and some of the most vital information to know. This travel guide will help you plan your St. Kitts and Nevis trip and make it a memorable and delightful experience.

CHAPTER 2

Nature and Wildlife

St. Kitts and Nevis, a twin-island republic in the Caribbean possesses a rich and diversified ecology and animals. The islands are home to a range of ecosystems, from volcanic mountains and rainforests to coral reefs and mangroves. The islands support a range of flora and animals, some of which are indigenous or endangered, such as the St. Kitts monkey, the Nevis turtle, and the national flower, the poinciana.

Some of the areas that you can visit to enjoy their nature and fauna are:

- The volcanic origins and the geology
- The rainforest, beaches, and coral reefs
- The flora and fauna of the islands
- Conservation efforts and eco-tourism

In this chapter, we will walk you through some of the Nature and wildlife sites to visit, such as the volcanic origins and the geology, The rainforest, beaches, and coral reefs, The flora and fauna of the islands, and much more.

The volcanic origins and the geology

St. Kitts and Nevis is a wonderful and amazing place for those who love to witness the strength and majesty of nature. The twin-island nation resulted from millions of years of volcanic activity that produced its rough environment, diversified ecosystems, and rich mineral riches. In this chapter, you will study the volcanic origins and the geology of St. Kitts and Nevis and how these shaped its history, culture, and attractions.

Volcanic origins

St. Kitts and Nevis are part of the Volcanic Caribbees, a band of islands that defines the eastern limit of the Caribbean Tectonic Plate1. The islands are the summits of a submerged mountain range generated by the subduction of the Atlantic Oceanic Plate under the Caribbean Plate. This process allowed magma to rise to the surface and erupt as volcanoes, producing islands throughout time. The islands are the summits of a submerged mountain range generated by the subduction of the Atlantic Oceanic Plate under the Caribbean Plate. This process allowed magma to rise to the surface and erupt as volcanoes, producing islands throughout time.

The oldest rocks in St. Kitts and Nevis are volcanic and sedimentary rocks from the Pliocene and Miocene epochs, dating back to 50 million years ago. The islands have witnessed multiple stages of volcanic activity since then, with the most recent eruptions happening in the Pleistocene Era, some 2 million years ago. The volcanoes of St. Kitts and Nevis are considered dormant, meaning they have not erupted in historical times, but they are still studied for signs of activity. The islands have witnessed multiple stages of volcanic activity since then, with the most recent eruptions happening in the Pleistocene Era, some 2 million years ago. The volcanoes of St. Kitts and Nevis are considered dormant, meaning they have not erupted in historical times, but they are still studied for signs of activity.

Geology

St. Kitts and Nevis have different geological features due to their differing ages and volcanic histories. St. Kitts is formed nearly primarily of volcanic rocks of andesite or dacite mineralogy, which are intermediate in composition between basalt and rhyolite. St. Kitts has a northwest-southeast direction, with a central mountain range that comprises three primary volcanic centers: Mount Liamuiga, Middle Island Range, and South East Peninsula Range. St. Kitts has a northwest-southeast direction, with a central mountain range that comprises three primary volcanic centers: Mount Liamuiga, Middle Island Range, and South East Peninsula Range.

Mount Liamuiga is the highest point of St. Kitts, with a height of 1,156 meters. It is also the youngest volcano on the island, with an age of less than 1 million years. It contains a big crater lake at its peak, surrounded by thick rainforest and home to different wildlife species. Mount Liamuiga is a famous place for trekking and birdwatching.

Middle Island Range is a range of eroded volcanic cones that run from Mount Liamuiga to Basseterre, the capital city of St. Kitts. The range features various historical structures, such as Brimstone Hill Fortress, a UNESCO World Heritage Site erected by the British in the 17th century to fight against French raids. The range also boasts spectacular views of the Caribbean Sea and the adjacent islands.

South East Peninsula Range is a small stretch of land that separates the Atlantic Ocean from the Caribbean Sea. 2 It is made of older volcanic materials that have been elevated and tilted by tectonic action. It is made of earlier volcanic materials raised and tilted by tectonic forces2. The range features some of the nicest beaches on St. Kitts, such as Frigate Bay, Banana Bay, and Cockleshell Bay. The range also features a salt pond that draws flamingos and other birds. The range features some of the nicest beaches on St. Kitts, such as Frigate Bay, Banana Bay, and Cockleshell Bay. The range also features a salt pond that draws flamingos and other birds.

Nevis is a single volcanic island that began its creation in the mid-Pliocene, some 3.45 million years ago. However, it features numerous eruptive foci ranging in age from mid-Pliocene to Pleistocene. The geology of Nevis can be split into four informal units:

- Volcanic rocks

- Volcanic rocks (pyroclastics and lahars)
- Fluviatile and lacustrine deposits (river and lake sediments)
- Elevated beaches

The most noticeable feature of Nevis is Nevis Peak, which rises to 985 meters above sea level. It is an active stratovolcano with a complex history of eruptions and collapses. It has a horseshoe-shaped crater on its southern face, which opens to the sea and produces a natural harbor named Charlestown Bay. Nevis Peak is covered by lush woodland and cloud forest, which provide habitat for numerous rare plants and animals.

The volcanic rocks on Nevis are predominantly made of ash, pumice, lapilli, and blocks that were ejected by explosive eruptions or deposited by volcanic mudflows (lahars). These rocks form steep slopes and valleys around Nevis Peak and mild flats along the coast. The volcanogenic rocks are rich in minerals such as gold, silver, copper, iron, lead, zinc, antimony, arsenic, mercury, and sulfur. Some of these minerals were mined in the past by European colonists.

The fluviatile and lacustrine deposits on Nevis are predominantly formed of sand, silt, clay, gravel, pebbles, cobbles, and boulders transported by rivers or collected in lakes. These deposits are located in the lowlands and coastal parts of Nevis, where they produce ideal soils for agriculture. The fluviatile and lacustrine strata also contain fossils of plants and animals that existed on Nevis in the past, including gigantic sloths, armadillos, monkeys, and rodents.

The raised beaches on Nevis are formed of coral reefs, shells, sand, and gravel that were uplifted by geological processes or sea level fluctuations. These beaches are found along the coast of Nevis, where they form cliffs, terraces, and platforms. The raised beaches are crucial for coastal erosion protection, as well as for tourism and enjoyment.

St. Kitts and Nevis is a fascinating site that highlights the glories of volcanic geology. The islands contain a range of landscapes, ecosystems, and resources that reflect their volcanic origins and history. By studying the volcanic origins and the geology of St. Kitts and Nevis, you will have a greater understanding of its natural beauty and cultural heritage. This guide to St. Kitts and Nevis 2023-2024 can aid you with having a wonderful journey to this Caribbean jewel.

The rainforest, beaches, and coral reefs

St. Kitts and Nevis are blessed with unique and spectacular natural environments, from the thick jungle that covers the volcanic mountains to the clean beaches that border the coast to the colorful coral reefs that teem with marine life. Here are some of the best spots to experience these wonders:

The rainforest

The rainforest of St. Kitts and Nevis is home to various flora and wildlife, such as monkeys, hummingbirds, orchids, and ferns. It also offers magnificent views, waterfalls, and hiking paths for nature enthusiasts and explorers. Some of the most popular rainforest attractions are:

Wingfield-Phillips Rain Forest Nature Walk: A delightful walk begins with broad fields and goes through the lush forest where tree frogs greet you in chorus. It takes roughly 2 hours to traverse the 3 kilometer-long path. It is located near Romney Manor, a historic sugar plantation now home to the Caribelle Batik, a local handicraft shop. The trail is open daily from 9 a.m. to 5 p.m. and costs $10 USD per person. The closest accommodation is Belle Mont

Farm, a premium eco-resort offering cottages, villas, and farmhouses with spectacular rainforest and sea views. The rates start from $450 USD per night.

Mount Liamuiga Volcano: The highest point on St. Kitts at 1,156 meters above sea level. It is an active volcano that features a crater lake at its top. It is a hard but rewarding climb that takes around 4 hours round trip. You need to take a guided trip to access the volcano, which is located on private territory. The tours cost roughly $80 per person, including transportation, a guide, an entrance charge, and refreshments. The closest lodging is Ottley's Plantation Inn, a historic plantation house converted into a delightful hotel with spacious rooms, gardens, pools, and a restaurant. The rates start from $250 USD per night.

Nevis Peak: Another volcanic mountain that rises 985 meters above sea level on Nevis. It offers a more difficult trek than Mount Liamuiga, comprising steep slopes and treacherous rocks. However, the panorama is equally magnificent, and you can see both St. Kitts and Nevis from the summit. You also need to take a guided trip to hike the summit, which is located on private territory. The tours cost roughly $100 per person, including transportation, a guide, an entrance charge, and refreshments. The closest lodging is Montpelier Plantation & Beach. This historic sugar plantation has been renovated into a luxury hotel with magnificent suites, pools, a spa, a tennis court, and a private beach. The rates start from $300 per night.

The beaches

St. Kitts and Nevis boast some of the most stunning beaches in the Caribbean, with white or black sand, clear or turquoise sea, calm or wavy waves, and isolated or vibrant atmospheres. You can enjoy swimming, sunbathing, snorkeling, surfing, kayaking, sailing on these beaches, or just relaxing with a drink or a meal at one of the beach bars or restaurants. Some of the most popular beaches are:

Frigate Bay South: A renowned beach in St. Kitts noted for its nightlife. It features white sand, blue ocean, and gentle waves, and it is flanked by hotels, restaurants, and pubs that offer live music, dancing, and entertainment. It is also the setting for some of the island's festivals and events, such as the St. Kitts Music Festival in June and the St. Kitts-Nevis National Carnival in December-January. The beach is open 24/7 and free to access. The closest hotel is St. Kitts Marriott Resort & The Royal Beach Casino, a luxury resort with rooms, suites, villas, pools, a spa, a golf course, a casino, and various eating options. The rates start from $200 per night.

Banana Bay Beach: An isolated beach on the south coast of St. Kitts. It features white sand, blue sea, and moderate waves, giving spectacular views of Nevis and the surrounding highlands. It is perfect for snorkeling, as it features a coral reef that hosts many fish and other aquatic species. It is also a fantastic site for watching sunsets and astronomy. The beach is available daily from sunrise to sunset and is free to enter. The closest hotel is Park Hyatt St. Kitts Christophe Harbour, a premium resort that features rooms, suites, villas, pools, a spa, a fitness center, and many dining options. The charges start from $500 per night.

Cockleshell Bay Beach: One of the most popular beaches on the southeast peninsula of St. Kitts. It features white sand, clean sea, and quiet waves, frequented by locals and visitors alike. It features a vibrant atmosphere, with music, games, and vendors selling food and drinks. It is also a fantastic site to watch the big leatherback turtles that nest on the beach from March to July. The beach is available daily from 9 a.m. to 6 p.m. and free to access. The closest hotel is Spice Mill, a charming and reasonably priced guesthouse that offers rooms and cottages with views of the ocean and a restaurant serving Caribbean and international cuisine. The rates start from $100 USD per night.

Pinney's Beach: The most famous beach on Nevis, on the west coast near Charlestown. It features white sand, turquoise sea, and gentle waves, and coconut trees and green hills back it. It is a long, wide beach with many areas for sunbathing, swimming, or playing. It also boasts various beach bars and restaurants, including the famed Sunshine's Bar, known for its Killer Bee rum punch and celebrity clientele. The beach is open 24/7 and free to access. The closest lodging is Four Seasons Resort Nevis, a luxury resort with rooms, suites, villas, pools, a spa, a golf course, a tennis court, and many dining options. The rates start from $400 per night.

Oualie Beach: A lovely beach on the north shore of Nevis. It features a white beach, clean water, and gentle waves, and it is great for families with children or beginners in water activities. It offers a multitude of sports, such as snorkeling, kayaking, sailing, windsurfing, kite surfing, and stand-up paddle boarding. It also offers a dive shop that can take you to some of the top diving areas around the island. The beach is available daily from 9 a.m. to 5 p.m. and free to access. The closest hotel is Oualie Beach Resort, a cozy and economical resort that has rooms with sea views and balconies, a pool, a spa, a restaurant, and a bar. The rates start from $150 per night.

Lover's Beach: A quiet beach on the north coast of Nevis. It boasts a white beach, turquoise ocean, and high waves, and it is great for couples who want quiet and romance. It is a hidden gem that may be accessed by a gravel road or a short walk from Oualie Beach. It has no facilities or services, so you must bring your food, drinks, and equipment. The beach is open 24/7 and free to access. The closest lodging is Nisbet Plantation Beach Club, a historic plantation house turned into a luxury hotel with big suites, gardens, pools, a spa, and a restaurant. The rates start from $300 per night.

The coral reefs

St. Kitts and Nevis boast some of the most diverse and lively coral reefs in the Caribbean, with more than 50 types of corals and hundreds of fish species and other marine life. The reefs are rich in history, including many shipwrecks and antiquities from the colonial past. You may explore these underwater treasures by diving, snorkeling, or joining a glass-bottom boat or submarine trip. Some of the most popular coral reef attractions are:

Booby High Shoals: A dive site on the south coast of Nevis that consists of multiple coral pinnacles that rise from 18 to 30 meters deep. It is called for the booby birds that nest on the neighboring rocks. It is one of the best spots to watch giant pelagic species, such as barracuda, tuna, wahoo, and shark. It also has several smaller species, such as angelfish, butterflyfish, and parrotfish. It is appropriate for advanced divers, as it has powerful currents and little visibility. You may schedule a diving tour with Scuba Safaris, a local dive outfit that visits several spots throughout Nevis daily. The tours cost roughly $100 per person, including transportation, a guide, equipment, and refreshments. The closest lodging is Paradise Beach Nevis, a premium resort that includes villas with private pools and beach access. The rates start from $600 per night.

Monkey Shoals: A diving location on the west coast of St. Kitts consists of multiple coral mounds ranging from 12 to 24 meters deep called after the monkeys who inhabit the neighboring island of Booby Island. It is one of the best spots to see beautiful corals, such as brain, star, and fan corals. The Monkey Shoals has some fish, such as grouper, snapper, and triggerfish. It is appropriate for intermediate divers, as it has moderate currents and adequate visibility. You may schedule a diving excursion with diving St. Kitts, a local dive shop that visits several spots throughout St. Kitts daily. The tours cost roughly $80 USD per person and include transportation, a guide, equipment, and refreshments. The closest lodging is Timothy Beach Resort, a quaint and economical resort that offers rooms and suites with sea views and balconies. The rates start from $120 each night.

Coconut Tree Reef: A snorkeling location on the south coast of St. Kitts, consisting of a shallow coral reef that spans from the shore to about 6 meters deep. It is named after the coconut trees that flourish along the beach. It is one of the best spots to witness a variety of corals, such as brain, elkhorn, and fire corals. It also has several fish, such as sergeant major, damselfish, and wrasse. The tree reef is great for novices and families, as it has calm water and high visibility. You may rent snorkeling gear from Blue Water Safaris, a local tour operator that offers snorkeling adventures, catamaran cruises, and island tours. The rental is roughly $10 per person and includes a mask, snorkel, fins, and vest. The closest accommodation is the Royal St. Kitts Hotel, a modern hotel that contains rooms, suites, studios, apartments, pools, a gym, a casino, and many eating options. The rates start from $150 per night.

The Caves: A dive destination on the north coast of Nevis that consists of a series of underwater caves and tunnels that are rich with marine life. The caves is named after the caverns that are visible from the surface. It is one of the best spots to see sponges, corals, lobsters, crabs, eels, and octopuses. It also has several fish, such as angelfish, butterflyfish, and parrotfish. It is appropriate for advanced divers, as it has powerful currents and little visibility. You may schedule a diving tour with Nevis Diving, a local dive outfit that visits several spots throughout Nevis daily. The tours cost roughly $90 per person, including transportation, a guide, equipment, and refreshments. The closest lodging is The Hermitage Plantation Inn, a historic plantation house that has been renovated into a delightful hotel with cottages, gardens, a pool, and a restaurant. The rates start from $200 per night.

To conclude, the rainforest, beaches, and coral reefs of St. Kitts and Nevis are some of the Caribbean's most attractive and diverse natural features. They offer many exploration, recreation, and relaxation options for guests of all ages and interests.

The flora and fauna of the islands

St. Kitts and Nevis are blessed with a rich and diversified natural heritage on land and in the water. The islands contain a diversity of tropical plants, animals, and marine life that will thrill nature lovers and eco-tourists. Here are some of the top locations to discover the island's flora and fauna:

Brimstone Hill Fortress National Park: The Brimstone are UNESCO World Heritage Site is a historical and architectural masterpiece and a shelter for animals. The park covers 15 hectares of forested hillside, where you can view birds, butterflies, monkeys, reptiles, and more. The park is open every day starting from 9:30 a.m. to 5:30 p.m. and the entrance price is US$15 for adults and US$7.50 for children. The closest hotel is the Sunset Reef St. Kitts, which offers 5-star accommodation with ocean views, an outdoor pool, a fitness center, and a garden. The fee per night is US$750.

Botanical   Gardens   of Nevis[https://www.botanicalgardennevis.com/]:   This gorgeous and serene oasis is full of tropical flowers and plants, orchid terraces, dolphin fountains, and water lily ponds. You can also visit the secret Rainforest Conservatory, where you can find ruins of an ancient temple and lovely flower treasures. The gardens are open everyday starting from 9:00 a.m. to 4:00 p.m; the entrance cost is US$13 for adults and US$8 for children. The closest hotel is the Four Seasons Resort Nevis, which provides contemporary villas with terraces, spa tubs, and garden or ocean views. The resort also offers a golf course, a spa, and three swimming pools. The fee each night is US$361.90.

St. Kitts wildlife – in pictures[https://www.theguardian.com/travel/gallery/2013/oct/01/st-kitts-wildlife-caribbean-in-pictures]: If you want to witness some of the most remarkable creatures that inhabit St. Kitts, you may check out this online gallery by The Guardian. It offers magnificent photographs of huge barracuda, flamingo tongue cowrie, vervet monkeys, Antillean crested hummingbirds, spiny lobster, and more. Additionally, you may discover some unique information about every species and its surroundings.

St. Kitts Nature & Wildlife Tours: If you want to experience the nature and wildlife of St. Kitts in person, you can join one of these tours that will take you to some of the best spots on the island. You can select from several choices, such as ATV trips, climbing in Mount Liamuiga (Volcano), scuba diving, boat cruising, fishing, yoga/meditation, paintball, and more. The rates vary depending on the tour type and duration.

St. Kitts and Nevis are blessed with a rich and diversified natural heritage on land and in the water. The islands contain a diversity of tropical plants, animals, and marine life that will thrill nature lovers and eco-tourists.

Conservation efforts and eco-tourism

St. Kitts and Nevis are two islands committed to protecting their natural environment and encouraging sustainable tourism. The islands contain various protected areas, conservation programs, and eco-friendly activities that display their biodiversity, heritage, and culture.

Protected areas

St. Kitts and Nevis have declared many national parks, nature reserves, or heritage sites to safeguard their natural and cultural values. Some of the most notable protected areas are:

Brimstone Hill Fortress National Park: Brimstone Hill Fortress is one of the UNESCO World Heritage Site that comprises a 17th-century British fortress erected on a volcanic hill overlooking the Caribbean Sea. The park also features a museum, a tourist center, and picturesque paths. The park is open daily from 9:30 a.m. to 5:30 p.m.; the admission charge is US$10 for adults and US$5 for children.

Central Forest Reserve National Park: This is a 3,800-hectare park that encompasses the central part of St. Kitts and preserves the island's largest remaining tract of tropical rainforest. Numerous indigenous and endangered species, including the St. Kitts vervet monkey, St. Kitts bullfinch, and St. Kitts orchid, may be found in the park. The park offers various hiking paths, such as the Olivees Mountain Trail, the Phillips Level Trail, and the Wingfield River Trail.

Nevis Peak National Park: This is a 985-hectare park that covers the Nevis Peak, the highest point on Nevis at 985 meters above sea level. The park offers beautiful views of the island and the surrounding sea and a hard trek to the summit. The park is accessible by guided excursions only, which can be organized through local operators, such as Sunrise excursions or Funky Monkey Tours.

Booby Island Nature Reserve: This is a small island off the northwest coast of Nevis that is a nesting location for hundreds of brown boobies, red-billed tropicbirds, and other seabirds. The island is also bordered by coral reefs that contain diverse aquatic life. The island is accessible by boat trips only, which can be arranged through local companies, such as Blue Water Safaris or Leeward Islands Charters.

Conservation initiatives

St. Kitts and Nevis have also undertaken various conservation projects to boost their environmental management and awareness. Some of the most notable conservation efforts are:

Improving Environmental Management through Sustainable Land Management: This is a GEF-funded project that aims to improve land use planning and management in St. Kitts and Nevis by updating the National Physical Development Plan, building codes, legal and regulatory frameworks, and digital capabilities. The initiative also comprises stakeholder discussions, capacity building, and awareness raising.

Conserving World Heritage through International Partnerships in Brimstone Hill Fortress National Park: This is a project that seeks to conserve the cultural and natural heritage of Brimstone Hill Fortress National Park by strengthening its management plan, improving its visitor facilities, enhancing its interpretation and education programs, and promoting its international recognition.

World Heritage Programme for Small Island Developing States (SIDS): This program aids St. Kitts and Nevis and other SIDS in finding, nominating, protecting, and managing their potential World Heritage sites. The initiative also encourages regional cooperation, knowledge exchange, and capacity building among SIDS.

Eco-tourism activities

St. Kitts and Nevis provide several eco-tourism activities that allow visitors to appreciate their natural beauty while minimizing their environmental impact. Some of the most popular eco-tourism activities are:

Ziplining: This activity involves gliding across the forest canopy on a succession of wires and platforms. It is a fun and exhilarating way to view the flora and fauna of St. Kitts and Nevis from a different perspective. There are two ziplining operators on St. Kitts: Sky Safari Tours and Zipline

St. Kitts. Both operate daily from 8:30 a.m. to 3:30 p.m. and charge roughly US$90 per person.

Snorkeling: This activity involves exploring the underwater world of St. Kitts and Nevis with a mask, snorkel, and fins. It is a pleasant and gratifying way to discover the coral reefs, fish, turtles, rays, and other marine species that inhabit the waters around the islands. There are various snorkeling locations on both islands, such as White House Bay, Shitten Bay, Pinney's Beach, Oualie Beach, and Booby Island. Some of them are accessible from shore, while others require a boat voyage. Numerous operators offer snorkeling tours, including Blue Water Safaris, Leeward Islands Charters, and Nevis Adventure Tours. The tours normally last 2 to 4 hours and cost US$50 to US$100 per person.

Hiking: This activity involves walking on routes that cross the varied landscapes of St. Kitts and Nevis. It is a demanding and rewarding way to experience the mountains, woods, valleys, waterfalls, and historical monuments that dot the islands. There are various hiking paths on both islands, such as the Olivees Mountain Trail, the Phillips Level Trail, the Wingfield River Trail, the Nevis Peak Trail, the Source Trail, and the Heritage Trail. Some are easy and suited for beginners, while others are complex and require assistance. Several operators offer hiking tours, such as Sunrise Tours, Funky Monkey Tours, and Oualie Beach Resort. The tours normally last 2 to 6 hours and cost US$40 to US$80 per person.

CHAPTER 3

Attractions and Activities

St. Kitts and Nevis,a twin-island republic in the Caribbean offers variety of sights and activities for vacationers. Whether you wish to explore the rich history and culture, appreciate the natural beauty and animals, or relax on the sandy beaches and turquoise waters, you will find something to fit your taste and budget. However, you are seeking some extra excitement and adventure. In that case, you can also attempt some exhilarating activities in St. Kitts and Nevis that will make your trip unforgettable.

In this travel guidebook, we will introduce you to the top sites and activities in St. Kitts and Nevis and give you some advice and recommendations on how to enjoy them. We will also give you some information on what to see and do on each island and some advice on how to design your schedule. This book will help you explore the great and different experiences that St. Kitts & Nevis offers.

Some of the sights and activities that we will discuss in this book are:

- The capital city of Basseterre and its landmarks
- The Brimstone Hill Fortress and its history
- The Romney Manor and the Caribelle Batik
- The scenic train and the sugar cane industry

These are just some of the highlights that await you in St. Kitts and Nevis. These islands have many more attractions and activities to discover and enjoy. This book will help you select the greatest ones to make your trip memorable.

The capital city of Basseterre and its landmarks

Basseterre is the capital and main city of St. Kitts and Nevis, located on the south coast of St. Kitts. It is a picturesque, historic city that blends colonial and modern architecture, culture, and commerce. It is also a gateway to the remainder of the island, as it has the primary airport, seaport, bus station, and tourism office. Here are some of the landmarks that you should not miss when visiting Basseterre:

Independence Square: The heart and spirit of Basseterre, where people and visitors meet to rest, socialize, and celebrate. The area was once known as the Pall Mall area, and it was the site of the slave market during the colonial era. Today, it is a tranquil and scenic park that has a fountain, a clock tower, a statue of Queen Victoria, and a memorial honoring St. Kitts and Nevis independence in 1983. The area is flanked by some of the city's oldest and most magnificent structures, such as the Anglican Cathedral of St. George, the Catholic Co-Cathedral of Immaculate Conception, the Government Headquarters, and the National Museum. The square is open 24/7 and free to access. The closest lodging is Ocean Terrace Inn, a small and economical hotel that offers rooms with sea views and balconies, a pool, a restaurant, and a bar. The rates start from $120 each night.

Berkeley Memorial Clock Tower: A significant landmark in the heart of the Circus, a roundabout based after the Piccadilly Circus in London. The clock tower was built in 1883 in honor of Thomas Berkeley Hardtman Berkeley, a formerly enslaved person who became a wealthy trader and politician. The clock tower includes four faces that show the time in different places, such as London, New York, Calcutta, and Basseterre. It also includes a water fountain used by humans and animals at its base. The clock tower is available 24/7 and free to access. The closest lodging is Bird Rock Beach Hotel, a modern hotel with rooms with sea views and balconies, a pool, a restaurant, and a bar. The rates start from $100 per night.

National Museum: A museum that highlights the history, culture, and natural heritage of St. Kitts and Nevis. The museum is housed in the Old Treasury Building, built in 1894 as the customs house and post office. The museum includes exhibits on numerous topics, such as the indigenous people, the colonial era, the sugar industry, slavery and emancipation, the independence movement, the festivals and events, the flora and fauna, and the arts and crafts. The museum also conducts lectures, workshops, and cultural performances yearly. The museum is open from Monday to Friday starting from 9 a.m. to 4 p.m. and on Saturday starting from 9 a.m. to 1 p.m. It costs $5 per person to enter. The closest accommodation is the Royal St. Kitts Hotel, a modern hotel that contains rooms, suites, studios, apartments, pools, a gym, a casino, and many eating options. The rates start from $150 per night.

Brimstone Hill Fortress: One of the UNESCO World Heritage Site that was formerly a British bastion against the French. It is located on the west coast of St. Kitts, roughly 15 kilometers from Basseterre. It is a large stronghold that was erected in the 17th and 18th centuries, employing limestone and volcanic rock. It features spectacular walls, bastions, cannons, barracks, and a museum that chronicles the castle's story and its participation in the fights between the European powers. It also gives panoramic views of the island and the sea. The stronghold is open every day starting from 9:30 a.m. to 5:30 p.m. and costs $10 per person to enter. The closest accommodation is Brimstone

Hill Fortress Lodge, a historic lodge that offers rooms with antique furnishings, gardens, and a café. The rates start at $80 each night.

Romney Manor: A former sugar plantation now home to the Caribelle Batik, a local handicraft shop that produces gorgeous fabrics utilizing wax-resist dying processes. It is located on the west coast of St. Kitts, about 10 kilometers from Basseterre. It is a tranquil and scenic area that boasts a 17th-century grand house, a 400-year-old saman tree, and a botanical garden that features tropical plants, flowers, and birds. You can observe a demonstration of how the batik is manufactured and buy some souvenirs for yourself or your loved ones. The house is open every day from 9 a.m. to 5 p.m. and costs $3 USD per person to enter. The closest hotel is Culture House, a small and economical guesthouse that offers rooms with sea views and balconies, a pool, and a restaurant. The rates start from $60 each night.

To summarize, the capital city of Basseterre and its landmarks are some of the most appealing and historic aspects of St. Kitts and Nevis. They offer a look into the colonial past and the modern culture of the islands. You can use this chapter as a guide to help you find the best sites to visit and enjoy in Basseterre. You can also check the latest weather forecasts, travel advisories, and COVID-19 protocols before you schedule your trip. Basseterre is a delightful and busy city that will welcome you with its beauty and charm.

The Brimstone Hill Fortress and its history

Perched on a mountaintop overlooking the Caribbean Sea, the Brimstone Hill Fortress National Park is a UNESCO World Heritage Site highlighting the British colonial era's military, technical, and architectural capabilities. Built by enslaved Africans over a century, the castle is one of the best-maintained ancient defenses in the Americas and gives breathtaking views of the surrounding islands and shoreline.

Address

Brimstone Hill Fortress National Park St. Thomas Middle Island Parish St. Kitts and Nevis

Opening hours

The stronghold is open daily from 9:30 a.m. until 5:30 p.m., except on Christmas Day and Good Friday.

How to get there

The stronghold is located about 10 miles (16 km) from Basseterre, the capital of St. Kitts and Nevis. You may reach it via vehicle, taxi, or bus. If you drive, follow the main road along the west coast of St. Kitts and look for the signs to Brimstone Hill. There is a parking area at the entrance to the park. If you take a cab, you can negotiate a round-trip cost with the driver or arrange a pick-up time for your return. If you take a bus, you can get one from Basseterre to Sandy Point Town and then walk or hitchhike for about 2 miles (3 km) to the park.

Prices

The admission price to the park is US$15 for adults and US$7.50 for children under 12 years old. The cost covers admission to the stronghold, the museum, the gift shop, and the facilities.

What to see and do

The stronghold consists of multiple bastions, barracks, magazines, artillery, and other features that demonstrate the strategic importance of St. Kitts in the 18th and 19th centuries. You can explore the site independently or take a guided tour that departs from the visitor center every hour. The tour lasts roughly 45 minutes and covers the history, architecture, and culture of the stronghold and its architects.

Some of the highlights of the fortress are:

The Citadel: The main fortification on Brimstone Hill's peak, where you can view the Monmouth Bastion, King's Bastion, King's Bastion, and Prince of Wales Bastion. The Citadel offers panoramic views over St. Kitts, Nevis, Sint Eustatius, Saba, and Montserrat.

The Museum: Housed in a former officer's quarters, the museum contains exhibits on the military, social, and natural history of Brimstone Hill and St. Kitts and Nevis. You may learn about the battles, sieges, treaties, slavery, emancipation, flora, and fauna that formed the island's past and present.

The Gift Store: Located next to the museum, the gift store carries souvenirs, books, maps, postcards, and local crafts you may take home as a memento of your visit.

The Picnic Area: Near the park entrance, there is a picnic area with tables, benches, and shade where you may rest and have a snack or a meal. There is also a vending machine that offers drinks.

Tips and advice

- Wear appropriate shoes, sunscreen, hat, and sunglasses as you will be walking on difficult terrain and exposed to the sun.

- Bring water and snacks, as the park has no restaurants or cafes.

- Please avoid touching or damaging any of the buildings or artifacts at the site out of respect for its historical and cultural value.

- Take photographs and videos for personal use only. Commercial photography or videography requires approval from the park management.

- Be mindful of your surroundings, and do not go off the marked trails or into restricted areas.

Closest hotel/accommodation

If you wish to stay near Brimstone Hill Fortress National Park, one of your alternatives is Sunset Reef St. Kitts, a 5-star hotel that faces the seashore in Ottley's town. The hotel offers spacious rooms with balconies, sea views, air conditioning, free Wi-Fi, flat-screen TVs, minibars and private bathrooms. The hotel offers guests with access to an outdoor pool, a fitness center, a garden, restaurant, and a bar. The hotel has a rating of 9.4 out of 10, based on 12 reviews from past guests. The price for a night's stay at Sunset Reef St. Kitts ranges from US$750 to US$1,250, depending on the season and availability.

The Brimstone Hill Fortress and its history is a fascinating part of the St. Kitts and Nevis tour guide that reveals the rich and diversified past of the island nation. Whether you are interested in military, engineering, architecture, culture, wildlife, or adventure, you will discover something to suit your taste and curiosity at this wonderful place. You will also discover the beauty and charm of the local sites that offer further opportunities to appreciate the scenery, history, and hospitality of St. Kitts and Nevis. The

Brimstone Hill Fortress is a must-see destination for those who want to experience the rich history of the Caribbean.

Romney Manor and Caribelle Batik

Romney Manor and Caribelle Batik are two of the most popular sites in St. Kitts, presenting a unique combination of history, culture, and art. Located on the grounds of the Wingfield Estate, the oldest surviving sugar plantation in the Caribbean, these sites showcase the legacy and ingenuity of the island.

Romney Manor

Romney Manor is a historic home that dates back to the 17th century when Sam Jeffreson II, the great-great-great-grandfather of Thomas Jefferson, the third president of the USA, owned it. The Earl of Romney eventually acquired the mansion, who renamed it and emancipated his enslaved Africans in 1834, becoming the first estate in St. Kitts to do so. The mansion has been converted into a museum featuring exhibits and artifacts related to the estate and the island's history.

The mansion is surrounded by eight acres of lush gardens that showcase a variety of tropical plants, flowers, and trees. The most amazing tree is a 400-year-old saman tree that covers half an acre with its branches. The gardens also contain:

- A bell tower that was used to signal slaves.
- A water wheel that powered the sugar mill.
- A petroglyph that attests to the existence of Amerindians.

Romney Manor is open daily from 9 a.m. to 5 p.m.; the admission cost is US$10 for adults and US$5 for children. The address is Old Road Town, St. Kitts.

Caribelle Batik

Caribelle Batik is a renowned batik studio and shop that operates on the property of Romney Manor. Batik is an old art style that includes producing motifs on fabric using wax and dye. Caribelle Batik offers unique and high-quality fabrics, garments, gifts, and accessories that reflect the colors and patterns of St. Kitts and Nevis.

At Caribelle Batik, you can observe live demonstrations of how batik is manufactured by professional artists who employ local cotton, silk, and rayon materials. You can also browse through the shop and purchase some of the gorgeous things that are manufactured on-site. You can get dresses, shirts, scarves, bags, wall hangings, cushions, tablecloths, and more.

Caribelle Batik is open daily from 9 a.m. to 5 p.m., with no admission fee2. The address is Old Road Town, St. Kitts.

Closest hotel/accommodation

The closest hotel/accommodation to Romney Manor and Caribelle Batik is Belle Mont Farm, a premium eco-resort on Kittitian Hill, a 400-acre organic farm and community. The resort provides access to hiking trails, golf courses, health facilities, farm-to-table cuisine, and spectacular views of the Caribbean Sea and nearby islands.

The resort has several types of lodging, such as cottages, villas, farmhouses, and guesthouses. All of them are spacious and comfortable, with king-sized mattresses, private pools or verandas, outdoor bathrooms, Wi-Fi, minibars, and more. The resort also provides complimentary breakfast baskets with fresh fruits, breads, jams, eggs, and juices.

The resort rating is 4.5 out of 5 stars, with a price range of US$500 to US$1,500 per night, depending on the season and the kind of Accommodation. The address is Belmont Resort Ltd., St. Paul's Parish, St. Kitts & Nevis.

Romney Manor and Caribelle Batik are two of the most popular sites in St. Kitts, presenting a unique combination of history, culture, and art.

The scenic train and the sugar cane industry

St. Kitts and Nevis is an island nation with a rich and violent past directly related to sugar cane production. For decades, the islands were the hub of the lucrative sugar trade, which impacted their economy, society, culture, and geography. Today, you can discover more about this intriguing piece of the islands' legacy by journeying on the St. Kitts Scenic Railway, one of the Caribbean's most distinctive and pleasant attractions.

The St. Kitts Scenic Railway

Experience the beauty of St. Kitts with a 3-hour tour on the St. Kitts Scenic Railway. This tour takes you on a 30-mile round trip around the island, with 18 miles on a narrow gauge train and 12 miles on a tourist bus. The railway was constructed from 1912 to 1926 to transport sugar cane from the estates to the mill located in Basseterre, the capital city. It provides a unique and historic view of the island. It was regarded as the "Last Railway in the West Indies" and ran until 2005 when the sugar business ended.

The train allows you to experience the island from a different perspective as you enjoy the spectacular views of

99

the ocean, the mountains, the rainforest, and the settlements. You will also learn about the history and culture of St. Kitts from your guide, who will point out the sights and give you stories along the journey. You will witness the remains of old sugar estates, windmills, chimneys, and bridges that testify to the island's past greatness. You will also witness the new developments that have transformed St. Kitts into a lively tourist destination.

The train consists of double-decker vehicles that feature an open-air upper level and an air-conditioned bottom level. Both levels include comfy seats and huge windows that allow you to appreciate the surroundings. The train also features a service bar that gives complimentary drinks and snacks and a souvenir shop that sells local crafts and items. The train has a state-of-the-art sound system that plays local music and commentary.

The bus half of the tour takes you to the south coast of St. Kitts, where you will view other sites such as Frigate Bay, Timothy Hill, Cockleshell Bay, and Majors Bay. You will also have an opportunity to stop at some gorgeous sites for photo opportunities.

The St. Kitts Scenic Railway operates every day from Monday to Saturday, with two departures per day: one in the morning and one in the afternoon. The journey starts and concludes at Needsmust Station, located close to the Robert L. Bradshaw International Airport. The tour costs $129 for adults and $64.50 for youngsters (ages 2-12). You can order your tickets online[http://www.stkittsscenicrailway.com/] or through your hotel or cruise ship.

Ocean Terrace Inn is the closest hotel to Needsmust Station, a 4-star hotel with a pool, restaurant, and bar. The average price per night is $150.

The Sugar Cane Industry

Sugar cane was introduced to St. Kitts by the French colonizers in the 17th century and soon became the principal crop of the island. The British also recognized the value of sugar cane and fought with the French for control of St. Kitts until 1713, when they achieved full command of it. Sugar cane was grown on huge plantations owned by wealthy landowners and worked by enslaved Africans. The sugar cane was processed into raw sugar, molasses, and rum at the sugar mills placed on each plantation.

The sugar industry was immensely profitable for St. Kitts, as it supplied the European market with high-quality sugar and rum. Cultivating sugar cane on the island required intensive labor, deforestation, irrigation, and fertilization, causing soil erosion, water pollution, and also depletion of natural resources which had negative impacts on the environment, society, culture, and politics. The plantation system also developed a rigid class structure based on race, wealth, and power, which led to social inequity, oppression, exploitation, resistance, and rebellion. The sugar industry also altered the island's culture, as it imported new languages, religions, cuisines, music, and art forms that merged European, African, and indigenous elements.

The sugar business fell in the 20th century due to several factors, such as competition from other sugar-producing countries, increased production costs, dropping market prices, and changing customer preferences. The government of St. Kitts and Nevis worked to diversify the economy by promoting tourism, industry, and services. Still, sugar remained many people's main Source of income and employment. The sugar business eventually terminated in 2005 after over 350 years of operation.

Today, you can still see the vestiges of the sugar business on the islands, as many of the historic plantations, mills, and estates have been conserved or converted into hotels, museums, or attractions. You can also learn more about the history and culture of the sugar business at numerous venues such as:

The St. Kitts Sugar Factory is the former sugar factory built in 1912 and functioning until 2005. It is a museum showcasing the machinery and equipment used to prepare sugar cane. You can also watch exhibits and videos that describe the history and significance of the sugar business on St. Kitts. The museum is located in Basseterre opposite Needsmust Station. The establishment is available for service on weekdays, Monday through Friday, from 9:00 a.m. until 4:00 p.m. The entrance price is $5 for adults and $2 for youngsters.

The Fairview Great Mansion & Botanical Garden: This is a renovated plantation mansion that dates back to the 18th century. It is a historical site that gives guided tours of the house and the garden. You may see the original furnishings and artifacts that belonged to the house's prior owners, as well as the kitchen, dining room, bedrooms, and bathrooms. You may also enjoy the magnificent views of Basseterre and Nevis from the veranda. The garden displays a variety of tropical plants and flowers utilized for food, medicine, or ornament. The house and garden are located in Boyds Village near Frigate Bay. They are open daily from 9:00 a.m. to 5:00 p.m. The entry price is $10 for adults and $5 for children.

The New River Estate: This sugar plantation has a long history, which dates back to the 17th century. It is now a historical site that retains the remnants of a sugar mill, a boiling house, a curing house, a distillery, and a lime kiln. You may also see a water wheel used to power the mill. The estate is located in New River near Gingerland on Nevis. It is open every day from 9:00 a.m. until 5:00 p.m. There is no entrance cost. However, donations are encouraged.

The picturesque railway and the sugar cane industry of St. Kitts and Nevis are two of the most interesting and fun ways to study the islands' history and culture. They provide a unique opportunity to experience the island from different angles as you travel by rail and bus along the coast and through the countryside. You will also learn about the stories and people that molded the islands' history and present them as you witness the relics and artifacts of the sugar trade that ruled the islands for centuries. Viewing the water, the mountains, the jungle, and the towns will leave you in awe of St. Kitts and Nevis' beauty and uniqueness. You will also enjoy the originality and ability of the local artists and artisans as you view their products and works along the road.

CHAPTER 4

Adventure and Sports

St. Kitts and Nevis is a place that offers numerous possibilities to explore and appreciate its natural and cultural features. Whether you want to experience the excitement of ziplining, hiking, diving, or sailing, explore the historical monuments and museums, or relax on the gorgeous beaches, you will discover a variety of adventure and sports alternatives to fit your requirements and interests. One benefit of visiting St. Kitts and Nevis is that it is simple to travel about since most of the sites are close to one another. You can choose from several modes of transportation, such as taxi, ferry, vehicle, bike, or even foot, depending on your money, time, and interest. Each transportation form has pros and downsides, so you may determine what works best for you. In this travel guidebook, we will present you with the numerous adventure and sports possibilities available in St. Kitts and Nevis and give you some advice and recommendations on how to use them. We will also give you some information on what to see and do in each area of St. Kitts and Nevis and some advice on planning your itinerary. We hope this guide will help you make the most of your trip and have a fantastic time in St. Kitts & Nevis.

The trekking trails and the Mount Liamuiga volcano

St. Kitts and Nevis island is a paradise for hikers who desire to discover the island nation's natural richness and beauty, St. Kitts and Nevis is a paradise. From lush rainforests to rough mountains, from calm waterfalls to spectacular views, there are hiking trails for every level of experience and interest. One of the most gratifying and demanding walks is the one to the summit of Mount Liamuiga, the tallest peak and the dormant volcano that dominates the scenery of St. Kitts.

Mount Liamuiga

Mount Liamuiga is a 1,156-meter (3,792-foot) stratovolcano in the northern part of St. Kitts. The highest point on the island of St. Kitts, in the federation of St. Kitts and Nevis, is a mountain that also happens to be one of the tallest peaks in the eastern Caribbean archipelago. This mountain is also the highest point in the entire British Leeward Islands. At the summit of the mountain is a 1-kilometer (0.6-mile) wide crater, which used to hold a small lake until 1959. However, as of 2006, the lake has re-formed in the crater. The latest proven eruptions from the volcano were roughly 1,800 years ago, but rumors of probable eruptions in 1692 and 1843 are deemed doubtful. Mount Liamuiga was formerly dubbed Mount Misery. The renaming occurred on the date of St. Kitts' independence, September 19, 1983. However, many older locals still refer to it as Mount Misery. Liamuiga is taken from the Kalinago name for the entire island of St. Kitts, which means "fertile land". The mountainsides are covered in farming and small communities up to 460 meters (1,500 feet), after which luxuriant tropical rainforests drape the slopes till cloud forest takes over at 900 meters (3,000 feet). Many trips and guided treks are scheduled to the peak's summit and surrounding rainforests, usually starting at Belmont Estate in the village of St. Paul's. From the peak, the views are magnificent, including the entire island and the lovely Caribbean Sea and the surrounding islands of Saba, Sint Eustatius, Saint Barthélemy, Saint Martin, Antigua, and Nevis.

Address

Belmont Estate St. Paul's St. Kitts

Opening hours

The hiking trail to Mount Liamuiga is open daily from sunrise to sunset.

How to get there

The hiking trail to Mount Liamuiga starts from Belmont Estate in St. Paul's hamlet, about 10 miles (16 km) from Basseterre, the capital of St. Kitts and Nevis. You may reach it via vehicle, taxi, or bus. If you drive, follow the main road along the west coast of St. Kitts and look for the signs to Belmont Estate or Mount Liamuiga Trailhead. A parking lot at Belmont Estate allows you to leave your car for a modest cost. If you take a cab, you can negotiate a round-trip cost with the driver or arrange a pick-up time for your return. If you take a bus, you may get one from Basseterre to St. Paul's village and then walk for about 15 minutes to Belmont Estate.

Prices

The hiking route to Mount Liamuiga is free. Still, you will need to pay an admission charge of US$5 per person to visit Belmont Estate, which includes access to its botanical gardens and historical buildings. You must also pay a guide charge to join a guided trek to the peak or the jungle. The guide cost varies based on the operator and the party size, but it normally runs from US$50 to US$100 per person. Some operators additionally include transportation, food, and beverages in their packages.

What to see and do

The hiking trek up Mount Liamuiga is one of the most spectacular and strenuous walks in St. Kitts and Nevis. It takes roughly 4 to 6 hours round-trip to accomplish the 5-mile (8-km) climb up and down the volcano. The absolute vertical ascend on this path is slightly over 2,380 feet (725 m), which is a good challenge for most hikers. This trek is not suggested for beginners or individuals with health difficulties. The track is generally straightforward to follow; however, it may be muddy, slippery, and steep in certain spots. You will need a guide to reach the peak or explore the jungle. You can:

Enjoy a journey through several habitats, from farmland to rainforest to cloud forest, and observe a variety of flora and creatures along the route, such as mango trees, orchids, ferns, monkeys, birds, and butterflies.

Reach the peak of Mount Liamuiga and marvel at the spectacular crater lake and the panoramic views of the island and the sea. You may even wander around the crater's rim or drop into it if you are daring.

Explore the forests surrounding the volcano and find its secrets, such as hidden waterfalls, streams, caverns, and animals. You may also learn about the history and culture of the volcano and its architects from your guide.

Have a picnic or a snack at one of the rest spots along the walk or peak, and enjoy the fresh air and the natural beauty of the surroundings.

Tips and guidance

- Wear appropriate shoes, sunscreen, hat, and sunglasses since you will be trekking over difficult terrain and exposed to the sun for many hours.

- Bring water and snacks since no eateries or cafés are inside the path.

- Book your guide in advance online or by phone to ensure your seat and prevent disappointment.

- Check the weather forecast before you travel since the path may be closed due to rain or lightning.

- Respect the ecological and cultural value of the place, and do not touch or destroy any of the flora or animals.

Other hiking paths

If you wish to explore more hiking routes in St. Kitts and Nevis, you may visit some of the following places:

Dos D'ane Pond / Verchilds Mountain Trail: The second-highest mountain on St. Kitts also provides a very tough trek, with > 2000 feet (600 m) vertical elevation rise and spectacular views of the island.

Valley of Giants Rainforest Trail: A simple 2-hour circle trek along a river in a spectacular rainforest valley. There's also an alternative ridge climb for the more daring.

Challengers Village - Bat Cave and Waterfall Trail: The principal highlights of this trek are self-explanatory. This easy to intermediate level climb takes roughly 4 to 5 hours.

Southern Peninsula Trail: This distinctive St. Kitts climb takes place near the south extremity of the island, giving 'dry scrub-brush terrain with access to unoccupied beaches and beautiful ocean vistas.

Nevis Mountain Trail: The tallest mountain on Nevis is a 3,232-foot (985 m) stratovolcano providing an extremely tough walk requiring climbing ropes and ladders. However, The views from the summit are worth it.

The Source + Waterfalls Trail: A moderate climb on Nevis that goes to a natural spring that provides water to most of the island and multiple waterfalls that are great for swimming.

Closest hotel/accommodation

If you wish to stay near Mount Liamuiga or other hiking trails in St. Kitts and Nevis, one of your alternatives is Belle

Mont Farm, a 5-star hotel set on a 400-acre organic farm on Kittitian Hill. The hotel provides large rooms with balconies, sea views, air conditioning, free Wi-Fi, flat-screen TVs, minibars, and private bathrooms with outdoor showers. The hotel also has a restaurant, a bar, a fitness center, a spa, a golf course, and an outdoor pool. The hotel has a rating of 9 out of 10. The fee for a night's stay at Belle Mont Farm varies from US$750 to US$1,250, depending on the season and availability.

Conclusion

The hiking paths and the Mount Liamuiga volcano in St. Kitts and Nevis are some of the greatest ways to explore the island nation's natural beauty, variety, and adventure. Whether searching for a pleasant walk, tough climb, peaceful swim, or exciting descent, you will discover a route that meets your taste and interest. You will also explore the flora and animals, the history and culture, and the people and stories that make St. Kitts and Nevis distinct and remarkable. The hiking trails and the Mount Liamuiga volcano in St. Kitts and Nevis are a must-do for anyone who loves nature, exploration, and fun.

Diving Sites and the Shipwrecks

St. Kitts and Nevis two are islands in the Caribbean that offer some of the region's most diverse and exciting diving experiences. You will find something to fit your taste and ability level, whether a novice or an expert. From beautiful coral reefs and marine life to historic shipwrecks and underwater caverns, there is much to explore and discover in these waters.

Coral Reefs

The coral reefs of St. Kitts and Nevis are home to various fish, turtles, rays, sharks, eels, lobsters, crabs, and more. You may experience the beauty and variety of these ecosystems at various depths and places. Some of the top reef dives are:

Coconut Tree Reef: One of the biggest reefs in the region, found off the south shore of St. Kitts. It has a depth range of 15 to 80 feet and comprises a wall, a slope, and a plateau with several coral formations and sponges. You may view barracudas, snappers, grunts, angelfish, parrotfish, trumpetfish, and more.

Monkey Shoals: Situated just off the western extremity of St. Kitts' peninsula between St. Kitts and Nevis. It has a depth range of 30 to 60 feet and comprises various coral heads and patches with sandy sections. You can observe nurse sharks, stingrays, turtles, moray eels, groupers, jacks, and more.

Sandy Point Reef: Located off the northwest coast of St. Kitts near Brimstone Hill Fortress. It has a depth range of 20 to 70 feet and displays a spur-and-groove formation with several nooks and overhangs. You can view lobsters, crabs, shrimps, octopuses, seahorses, frogfish, scorpionfish, and more.

Shipwrecks

More than 400 ships have fallen off the coasts of St. Kitts and Nevis, with just a dozen or so being recognized to date2. The most popular shipwreck dives are:

MV River Taw: The 144-foot inter-island freighter was destroyed in 1985 in Frigate Bay on the south coast of St. Kitts. It rests in around 50 feet of water and is separated into two portions by Hurricane Hugo in 1989. The wreck's coral and sponge cover attracts schools of fish, barracudas, turtles, rays, and other marine life.

MV Talata: The 180-foot ship was destroyed in 1983 at Basseterre Bay on the southwest coast of St. Kitts. It rests upright in approximately 60 feet of water on a reef with a sandy bottom. The wreck is mainly intact and has multiple opportunities for entry. You may observe jacks, snappers, grunts, angelfish, parrotfish, trumpetfish, moray eels, lionfish, and more.

MV Corinthian: The 140-foot tugboat was destroyed in 1995 at Sandy Point on the northwest coast of St. Kitts. It rests upright in approximately 60 feet of water on a sandy floor with a reef nearby. The wreck is almost clean and has several elements to investigate, such as the wheelhouse, the engine room, and the propeller. You may view rays, flounders, groupers, puffers, porcupinefish, and more.

Caves

If you are searching for something more daring and hard, you might try diving into some of the underwater caverns near St. Kitts and Nevis. These caverns are tough for the faint-hearted since they need strong buoyancy control, navigation abilities, and specific equipment like lights and reels. Some of the greatest cave dives are:

Black Coral Cave: Located off the southeast coast of Nevis near Pinney's Beach. It has a depth range of 40 to 100 feet and comprises a network of tunnels and chambers leading to a big cavern with black coral trees.

Nags Head Cave: Located off the northeast coast of St. Kitts near Nags Head Point. It has a depth range of 40 to 80 feet and comprises a lengthy tunnel that opens into a dome-shaped chamber with stalactites and stalagmites.

Booby High Shoals Cave: Located off the northwest coast of Nevis near Booby Island. It has a depth range of 50 to 90 feet and comprises a tiny crack that extends into a vast chamber with a sandy bottom and a vertical exit.

How to Get There

The simplest method to go to St. Kitts and Nevis is via aircraft. Direct flights are from the US, Canada, UK, and other Caribbean islands to Robert L. Bradshaw

International Airport on St. Kitts and Vance W. Amory International Airport on Nevis. You may also take a ferry or a water taxi between the two islands, which takes around 45 minutes.

To access the diving spots, contact a dive company offering boat transportation, equipment rental, guides, and safety procedures. Various diving operations on both islands provide varying packages and pricing based on the season, the amount of dives, and the degree of expertise. Some of the more respected diving operators are:

Dive St. Kitts: Located at the Bird Rock Beach Hotel on the south coast of St. Kitts. It provides daily dives to all the main sites surrounding St. Kitts and Nevis and night dives, wreck dives, cave dives, and specialty courses. It boasts a fleet of three custom-built diving boats and a crew of skilled and pleasant employees.

Kenneth's Dive Centre: Located at Oualie Beach on the northwest coast of Nevis. It provides daily dives to all the main sites surrounding Nevis and St. Kitts, night dives, wreck dives, cave dives, and specialty courses. It boasts a fleet of two roomy diving boats and a crew of skilled and trained employees.

Pro Divers St. Kitts: Located at the St. Kitts Marriott Resort on the southeast coast of St. Kitts. It provides daily dives to all the main sites surrounding St. Kitts and Nevis and night dives, wreck dives, cave dives, and specialty courses. It boasts a fleet of two contemporary diving boats and a crew of qualified and motivated employees.

When to Go

The best time to go diving in St. Kitts and Nevis is from December to May. During this time, the weather is dry and sunny, the water is calm and clear, and the visibility is good. The typical water temperature is approximately 80°F (27°C) year-round, so you only need a 3mm wetsuit or less.

The worst season to dive in St. Kitts and Nevis is from June to November when the weather is damp and windy, the water is choppy and muddy, and the visibility is low. This is also the hurricane season, so there is a danger of storms and cancellations.

Prices

The rates for diving in St. Kitts and Nevis vary based on the dive operator, the season, the number of dives, and the degree of expertise. Generally speaking, a two-tank dive will cost you around $100, $150 for a three-tank dive, $200 for a four-tank dive, $50 for a night dive, $75 for a wreck dive or a cave dive, $300 for an open water course, $400 for an advanced open water course, $500 for a rescue diver course, and $800 for a divemaster course.

These rates normally include boat transportation, equipment rental, guides, taxes, and fees. However, some dive operators may charge extra for products like nitrox fills, dive computers, cameras, lights, reels, etc. You may also choose to tip your guide or crew if you are happy with their service.

Accommodation

Several hotel alternatives on both islands suit different budgets and interests. Some of the better hotels near the diving destinations are:

Bird Rock Beach Hotel: A three-star hotel on the south coast of St. Kitts near Dive St. Kitts. It features 46 rooms with balconies overlooking the ocean or the garden, a restaurant, a bar, a pool, a spa, a gym, a tennis court, and free Wi-Fi. The prices start at $120 per night.

Oualie Beach Resort: A three-star resort on the northwest coast of Nevis near Kenneth's Dive Centre. It features 32 rooms with verandas overlooking the beach, a restaurant, a bar, a pool, a spa, a bike rental store, and free Wi-Fi. The prices start at $150 per night.

St. Kitts Marriott Resort & The Royal Beach Casino: A four-star resort on the southeast coast of St. Kitts near Pro Divers St. Kitts. It offers 389 rooms with balconies or patios overlooking the ocean or the golf course, a casino, eight restaurants, three bars, three pools, a spa, a gym, a golf course, and free Wi-Fi. The costs start at $200 per night.

The diving locations and the shipwrecks of St. Kitts and Nevis are a must-see for any diver who wishes to appreciate the beauty and history of the Caribbean. Whether searching for bright coral reefs, historic shipwrecks, or daring caverns, you will find something to fit your taste and ability level. You may also enjoy the warm and clear water, the friendly and professional dive operators, and the pleasant and convenient lodging alternatives. St. Kitts and Nevis are a diver's paradise.

The golf courses and the cricket matches

In St. Kitts and Nevis, there are many opportunities to play golf and cricket, if you love these sports. The island country features two world-class golf courses that provide breathtaking vistas and demanding layouts and a bustling cricket culture that highlights the passion and skill of the local players and spectators.

Golf courses

St. Kitts and Nevis features two golf courses that appeal to various levels of talent and money. Both are situated on the islands' west coast, overlooking the Caribbean Sea.

Royal St. Kitts Golf Club

The Royal St. Kitts Golf Club is an 18-hole, par-71 course that stretches 6,900 yards from the back tees. It is one of the few courses with holes in the Atlantic and Caribbean oceans. The course was built by Canadian architect Thomas McBroom, who redesigned it in 2004 to improve its natural beauty and strategic difficulty. The course has broad fairways, big greens, 83 bunkers, and 12 lakes. It also gives amazing views of the neighboring mountains, beaches, and islands.

Address

Zenway Blvd, Lucas, Saint Kitts

Opening hours

The course is available daily from 6:30 a.m. to 6:30 p.m., except on Christmas Day and Good Friday.

How to get there

The course is situated approximately 10 miles (16 km) from Basseterre, the capital of St. Kitts and Nevis. You may reach there via vehicle, taxi or bus. If you drive, take the main road along the west coast of St. Kitts and look for the signs to Royal St. Kitts Golf Club. There is a parking area at the entrance of the club. If you take a cab, you may negotiate a round-trip cost with the driver or schedule a pick-up time for your return. If you take a bus, you may get one from Basseterre to Frigate Bay and then walk for approximately 15 minutes to the club.

Prices

The green fee for 18 holes is US$165 in peak season (December to April) and US$140 in low season (May to November). The cost includes a golf cart and access to the practice facilities. There are discounts for Marriott Hotel and Marriott Vacation Club members and tee times after 12:00 p.m. or 2:00 p.m. Rental clubs are available for US$65 for 18 holes or US$45 for 9 holes.

What to see and do

The Royal St. Kitts Golf Club provides various services and facilities for players and non-golfers. You can:

- Enjoy a game of golf on one of the most gorgeous and demanding courses in the Caribbean.

- Use the putting green, chipping area, or driving range to perfect your swing.

- Take a lesson with a PGA-certified professional instructor.

- Store for golf equipment, gear, and souvenirs at the pro store.

- Dine at one of the two on-site restaurants: The Grille at Royal St. Kitts Golf Club or The Calypso Restaurant.

- Relax at the clubhouse lounge or patio, where you may enjoy beverages, nibbles, and live entertainment.

- Pamper yourself at the Emerald Mist Spa, which provides massages, facials, manicures, pedicures, and more.

- Stay at the Marriott Resort & The Royal Beach Casino, which is close to the golf club and provides exquisite accommodations, suites, and villas with sea views, a casino, a pool, a fitness center, and more.

Tips and guidance

- Wear suitable golf clothes, such as collared shirts, slacks or shorts (no jeans or denim), and soft-spiked shoes.

- Bring sunscreen, a hat, sunglasses, and a drink since you will be exposed to the sun for many hours.

- Book your tee time in advance online or by phone to reserve your favorite spot.

- Check the weather forecast before you go since the course may shut due to rain or lightning.

- Respect the rules and etiquette of golf, and do not annoy other players or damage the course.

Four Seasons Golf Course

The Four Seasons Golf Course is an 18-hole, par-71 course that covers 6,766 yards from the back tees. It is situated on the island of Nevis, near the Four Seasons Resort Nevis. The course was created by Robert Trent Jones II, who integrated the island's natural elements into his layout. The route travels through beautiful jungles, coconut plantations, and old sugar cane farms. It also provides beautiful views of Mount Nevis, Pinney's Beach, and St. Kitts.

Address

Pinney's Beach, Nevis

Opening hours

The course is available every day from 7:00 a.m. until 6:00 p.m.

How to get there

The course is around 6 miles (10 km) from Charlestown, the capital of Nevis. You may reach there via vehicle, taxi or bus. If you drive, take the main road down the west coast of Nevis and look for the signs to Four Seasons Resort Nevis. There is a parking area at the entrance to the resort. If you take a cab, you may negotiate a round-trip cost with the driver or schedule a pick-up time for your return. If you take a bus, you can get one from Charlestown to Pinney's Beach and walk for approximately 10 minutes to the resort.

Prices

The green fee for 18 holes is US$230 in peak season (December to April) and US$190 in low season (May to November). The cost includes a golf cart and access to the practice facilities. There are special deals for Four Seasons

Resort Nevis guests and tee times after 12:00 p.m. or 2:00 p.m. Rental clubs are available at US$85 per day. Driving range balls are offered for US$75 with clubs or US$25 without clubs.

What to see and do

The Four Seasons Golf Course provides various services and facilities for players and non-golfers. You can:

- Enjoy a game of golf on one of the most gorgeous and demanding courses in the Caribbean.

- Practice your swing at the driving range, putting green, or chipping area.

- Take a lesson with a PGA-certified professional instructor.

- Store for golf equipment, gear, and souvenirs at the pro store.

- Dine at one of the three on-site restaurants: Mango, Coral Grill, or Cabana.

- Relax at the clubhouse lounge or patio, where you may enjoy beverages, nibbles, and live entertainment.

- Pamper yourself at the Spa at Four Seasons Resort Nevis, which provides massages, facials, body treatments, salon services, and more.

- Stay at the Four Seasons Resort Nevis, close to the golf course and provides exquisite accommodations, suites, and villas with sea views, a pool, a fitness center, a tennis court, and more.

Tips and guidance

- Wear suitable golf clothes, such as collared shirts, slacks or shorts (no jeans or denim), and soft-spiked shoes.

- Bring sunscreen, a hat, sunglasses, and a drink since you will be exposed to the sun for many hours.

- Book your tee time in advance online or by phone to reserve your favorite spot.

- Check the weather forecast before you go since the course may shut due to rain or lightning.

- Respect the rules and etiquette of golf, and do not annoy other players or damage the course.

Cricket matches

Cricket is more than simply a sport in St. Kitts and Nevis; it is a way of life. The island country has a strong, cricketing history and culture that extends back to the colonial days. Cricket is played at all levels, from school children to national teams. The island country also holds international cricket matches and tournaments that draw some of the world's top players and teams.

Warner Park

Warner Park is the principal cricket facility in St. Kitts and Nevis. It is situated in Basseterre, the capital of St. Kitts and Nevis. It has a capacity of 8,000 spectators with a new pavilion with dressing rooms, media facilities, VIP lounges, and more. The venue has held various international cricket matches since 2006, including Test matches, One Day Internationals (ODIs) and Twenty20 Internationals (T20Is). It also hosts domestic cricket matches and competitions like the Leeward Islands Cricket Tournament and the St. Kitts Cricket Association Premier League.

Address

Lozack Road, Basseterre

Opening hours

The ground is open whenever a cricket match or event occursHow to get there

The ground is roughly 1 mile (1.6 km) from downtown Basseterre. You may reach there via vehicle, taxi or bus. If you drive, take the main road down the south coast of St. Kitts and look for the signs to Warner Park. There is a parking lot at the entrance to the ground. If you take a cab, you may negotiate a rate with the driver or schedule a pick-up time for your return. If you take a bus, you may get one from downtown Basseterre to Lozack Road and then walk for approximately 5 minutes to the ground.

Prices

The admission fees vary based on the kind and quality of cricket matches or events at Warner Park. Generally, they vary from US$5 to US$50 per person daily. You may purchase tickets online or at the box office at Warner Park.

What to see and do

Warner Park provides an exciting and enjoyable experience for cricket enthusiasts and newbies. You can:

- Watch some of the world's top cricket players and teams engage in spectacular matches and tournaments.

- Cheer for your favorite club or player, or join the local supporters in supporting the St. Kitts and Nevis Patriots, the Caribbean Premier Competition (CPL) home team, a professional T20 cricket competition involving six franchises throughout the region.

- Enjoy the joyful atmosphere and the exciting music, dancing, and cuisine that accompany every cricket match or event at Warner Park.

- Learn more about the history and culture of cricket in St. Kitts and Nevis and the exploits and contributions of the local cricket legends, such as Sir Vivian Richards, Elquemedo Willett, Stuart Williams, and Runako Morton.

- Participate in cricket clinics, coaching sessions, camps, or tours that different organizations and operators at Warner Park give.

Tips and guidance

- Wear comfortable clothes, sunscreen, a hat, and sunglasses since you will be exposed to the sun for many hours.

- Bring water and snacks since there are few alternatives for food and beverages under the ground.

- Book your tickets in advance online or by phone to reserve your seat and avoid lengthy lineups at the box office.

- Check the schedule and the weather prediction before you travel since the matches or activities may be postponed or canceled due to rain or other circumstances.

- Respect the rules and etiquette of cricket, and do not interfere with the players, umpires, or other fans.

Other cricket venues

If you wish to explore more cricket venues in St. Kitts and Nevis, you may visit some of the following places:

Conaree Cricket Centre: A cricket facility that conducts domestic cricket matches and tournaments and training sessions for local players. It is situated in Conaree Village, approximately 4 miles (6 km) from Basseterre. It has a capacity of 2,000 spectators with a pavilion with dressing rooms, media facilities, VIP lounges, and more.

Molineux Cricket field: A cricket field that holds domestic cricket matches, competitions, and community activities. It is in Molineux Village, approximately 5 miles (8 km) from Basseterre. It has a capacity of 1,500 spectators with a pavilion with dressing rooms, media facilities, VIP lounges, and more.

Nevis Recreation field: A cricket field that holds local cricket matches and competitions, as well as international cricket matches on occasion. It is situated in Charlestown, the capital of Nevis. It has a capacity of 3,000 spectators with a pavilion with dressing rooms, media facilities, VIP lounges, and more.

Closest hotel/accommodation

If you wish to stay near Warner Park or other cricket fields in St. Kitts and Nevis, one of your alternatives is Ocean Terrace Inn, a 4-star hotel that overlooks Basseterre Bay. The hotel provides large rooms with balconies, sea views, air conditioning, free Wi-Fi, flat-screen TVs, minibars and private bathrooms. The hotel also has a garden, a restaurant, a bar, and an outdoor pool. The hotel has a rating of 8.6 out of 10. The price for a night's stay at Ocean

Terrace Inn varies from US$200 to US$300, depending on the season and availability.

Conclusion

The golf courses and the cricket matches in St. Kitts and Nevis are some of the greatest ways to explore the island nation's natural beauty, cultural variety, and sports passion. Whether you are a novice, pro, spectator, or participant, you will find something to fit your taste and interest at these places. You will also discover the kindness and charm of the local people, who will welcome you with open arms and make you feel at home. The golf courses and the cricket matches in St. Kitts and Nevis are a must-do for everyone who likes sports, adventure, and enjoyment.

Ziplining, kayaking, and sailing

St. Kitts and Nevis are islands that provide a range of adventure activities that enable you to appreciate their natural beauty from diverse angles. Whether you want to fly over the forest canopy, paddle along the coast, or sail across the sea, you will find many alternatives to fit your interests and talents.

Ziplining

Ziplining is a sport that includes gliding across the forest canopy on a succession of wires and platforms. It is a fun and thrilling way to view the beauty and animals of St. Kitts and Nevis from a fresh perspective. You will experience spectacular views of the mountains, valleys, rivers, and ocean as you zoom from one station to another.

There are two ziplining companies in St. Kitts: Sky Safari Tours and Zipline St. Kitts. Both run daily from 8:30 a.m. to 3:30 p.m. and charge roughly US$90 per person. Both need a minimum age of 7 and a maximum weight of 275 lbs. Both include safety equipment, training, and transportation from your hotel or cruise ship.

Sky Safari Tours provides four zip lines ranging from 135 to 800 feet in length and 25 to 250 feet in height. The longest zipline is dubbed The Boss and reaches speeds of up to 80 km/h. The trip lasts around two hours and includes visiting the historic Wingfield Estate and Romney Manor.

Zipline St. Kitts provides five zip lines ranging from 250 to 1,350 feet in length and 50 to 250 feet in height. The longest zipline is dubbed The Screamer and reaches speeds of up to 100 km/h. The trip lasts roughly three hours and includes visiting the picturesque Timothy Hill.

Kayaking

Kayaking is an activity that includes exploring the aquatic environment of St. Kitts and Nevis using a kayak, a small boat driven by paddles. It is a pleasant and gratifying way to explore the coral reefs, fish, turtles, rays, and other marine species that inhabit the seas surrounding the islands. You may also enjoy the sights of the coastline, beaches, and hills as you paddle around.

There are various kayaking operators on both islands, such as Blue Water Safaris, Leeward Islands Charters, Nevis

Adventure Tours, Oualie Beach Resort, and St. Kitts Water Sports. They provide many varieties of kayaks, such as single, double, sit-on-top, or glass-bottomed. They also give safety equipment, teaching, and assistance.

The kayaking experiences normally run for two to four hours, costing from US$50 to US$100 per participant. They frequently include snorkeling stops at some of the greatest sites on both islands, such as White House Bay, Shitten Bay, Pinney's Beach, Oualie Beach, and Booby Island. Some of them also offer lunch or drinks.

Sailing

Sailing is an activity that includes traveling across the sea aboard a sailboat or a catamaran. It is a magnificent and romantic way to explore the beauty and ambiance of St. Kitts and Nevis. You may relax on the deck, swim in the clean water, snorkel among the colorful reefs, or watch the sunset over the horizon.

There are several sailing operations on both islands, such as St.Kitts Yacht Charters, Half Tidy Luxury Yacht Charter, Caribbean Yacht Adventures, Blue Water Safaris, Leeward

Islands Charters, and Belle Mont Farm. They provide several sailboats or catamarans, such as parasailing, scuba diving, taxi, or adventure trips. They also offer safety equipment, teaching, and entertainment.

The sailing trips normally run for two to six hours, costing from US$100 to US$500 per person. They frequently include snorkeling stops at some of the greatest sites on both islands, including Frigate Bay, South Friars Bay, Cockleshell Bay, Oualie Beach, and Booby Island. Some of them even include lunch or supper.

Closest hotel/accommodation

The nearest hotel/accommodation to these activities depends on the island you are staying on. If you are vacationing on St. Kitts, you may select from various choices around Basseterre or Frigate Bay, such as:

Park Hyatt St. Kitts Christophe Harbour: This is a five-star resort that provides magnificent rooms and suites with ocean views, private pools or patios, Wi-Fi, minibars, and more. The resort is equipped with a spa, a fitness center, two pools, three restaurants, and a bar. This resort has a rating of 4.5 out of 5 stars, with a price range of US$500 to US$1,000 per night, depending on the season and the kind of Accommodation. The location is Banana Bay, South East Peninsula, Parish of St. George, St. Kitts.

Royal St. Kitts Hotel: This is a four-star hotel that provides contemporary rooms and suites with garden or ocean views, kitchenettes, Wi-Fi, cable TV, and more. The hotel offers a variety of amenities including a golf course, two pools, a gym, a restaurant, and a bar. The hotel has a rating of 4 out of 5 stars with a price range of US$200 to US$400 a night, depending on the season and the kind of Accommodation. The address is 858 Frigate Bay Road, Frigate Bay, St. Kitts.

If you are vacationing on Nevis, you may select from various alternatives around Charlestown or Oualie Beach, such as:

Four Seasons Resort Nevis: This is a five-star resort that provides large rooms and suites with ocean or mountain views, balconies or patios, Wi-Fi, minibars, and more. The resort also provides a spa, a fitness center, three pools, four restaurants, and two bars. The resort's rating is

4.5 out of 5 stars, with a price range of US$600 to US$1,200 per night, depending on the season and the Accommodation type. The address is Pinney's Beach, Charlestown, Nevis.

Oualie Beach Resort: This is a three-star resort that provides charming rooms and cottages with beachfront views, Wi-Fi, cable TV, and more. The resort also offers a spa, a diving center, a restaurant, and a bar. The resort has a rating of 4 out of 5 stars and a price range of US$150 to US$300 per night, depending on the season and the kind of Accommodation. The address is Oualie Beach Road 1, Oualie Bay.

CHAPTER 5

Accommodation and Dining

Welcome to St. Kitts and Nevis, a location offering everyone something. Whether searching for a comfortable and beautiful hotel, a quaint and lovely inn, a practical and handy apartment, or an exciting and adventurous camping site, you will discover a selection of accommodation alternatives that meet your requirements and interests. One of the perks of visiting St. Kitts and Nevis is that you will never run out of places to eat since most restaurants and cafés are nearby. Depending on your budget, taste, and mood, you may experience diverse cuisines, such as local, Caribbean, international, or fusion. Each cuisine has peculiarities and tastes, so you may select what fits you best.

In this travel guidebook, we will show you the many hotels and eating alternatives available in St. Kitts and Nevis and offer suggestions and advice on how to utilize them. We will also provide you with some information on what to see and do in each location of St. Kitts and Nevis and some advice on organizing your schedule. We expect this chapter will help you find suitable Accommodation for your stay and lead you to a delightful time in St. Kitts and Nevis.

Hotels, Resorts, and Villas

St. Kitts and Nevis are two stunning and beautiful islands in the Caribbean that provide a choice of lodging alternatives for varied budgets and interests. Whether searching for a luxurious resort, a comfortable hotel, or a private villa, you will find something to fit your taste and requirements. Here are some of the best hotels, resorts, and villas on both islands.

St. Kitts

St. Kitts is the larger and more developed of the two islands, with more Accommodation choices. Most of the hotels and resorts are located on the south coast, near Frigate Bay and Basseterre, where you can enjoy the beach, the golf course, the casino, and the nightlife. Some of the best hotels and resorts in St. Kitts are:

St. Kitts Marriott Resort & The Royal Beach Casino: A four-star resort on the southeast coast of St. Kitts near Pro Divers St. Kitts. It offers 389 rooms with balconies or patios overlooking the ocean or the golf course, a casino, eight restaurants, three bars, three pools, a spa, a gym, a golf course, and free Wi-Fi. The costs start at $200 per night.

Royal St. Kitts Hotel: A four-star hotel on the south coast of St. Kitts near Frigate Bay Beach. It has a restaurant, a bar, two pools, a fitness center, a golf course, and 215 rooms consisting of balconies or patios overlooking the ocean, the pool, or the garden. There is also free Wi-Fi available. The prices start at $179 per night.

Bird Rock Beach Hotel: A three-star hotel on the southwest coast of St. Kitts near Basseterre. It features 46 rooms with balconies overlooking the ocean or the garden, a restaurant, a bar, a pool, a spa, a gym, a tennis court, and free Wi-Fi. The prices start at $95 per night.

If you want a more quiet and personal atmosphere, rent a villa in St. Kitts. Some of the greatest villas on St. Kitts are:

Sunset Reef St. Kitts: A five-star villa on the north shore of St. Kitts near Ottley's Plantation Inn. It contains four bedrooms with en-suite bathrooms, a living room, a dining room, a kitchen, a laundry room, a terrace, a pool, a jacuzzi, a grilling area, and free Wi-Fi. The charges start at $750 per night.

Belle Mont Farm: A four-star property on the northwest coast of St. Kitts near Dieppe Bay Town. It contains three bedrooms with en-suite bathrooms, a living room, a dining room, a kitchen, a laundry room, a balcony, a pool, a spa tub, a fire pit, and free Wi-Fi. The charges start at $600 per night.

Ocean Song Villa: A three-star villa on the southeast coast of St. Kitts near Turtle Beach. It offers two bedrooms with en-suite bathrooms, a living room, a dining room, a kitchen, a laundry room, a terrace, a pool, a grilling area, and free Wi-Fi. The costs start at $300 per night.

Nevis

Nevis is the smaller and quietest of the two islands, with fewer options for lodging. Most hotels and resorts are on the west coast, between Charlestown and Pinney's Beach, where you can experience the colonial beauty, the botanical gardens, and the local food. Some of the greatest hotels and resorts on Nevis are:

Four Seasons Resort Nevis: A five-star resort on the northwest coast of Nevis near Pinney's Beach. It features 196 rooms and homes with air conditioning, TVs with DVD players, telephones, marble bathrooms with hairdryers, verandas overlooking the beach or the mountains, three infinity pools, spa facilities, a golf course, four restaurants, a library bar, and free Wi-Fi. The prices start at $361.90 per night.

The Hamilton Beach Villas & Spa: A four-star resort on the west coast of Nevis near Pinney's Beach. It features 79 rooms and villas with air conditioning, TVs with cable channels, telephones, kitchens with microwaves and refrigerators, balconies overlooking the ocean Mount Nevis, numerous pools, tropical gardens, a beachfront restaurant, a bar, and free Wi-Fi. The prices start at $150 per night.

Montpelier Plantation & Beach: A four-star resort on the northeast coast of Nevis near Charlestown. It features 19 rooms and suites with air conditioning, TVs with DVD players, telephones, bathrooms with hairdryers, patios overlooking the garden or the ocean, a pool, a spa, a tennis court, a private beach, three restaurants, a bar, and free Wi-Fi. The prices start at $295 per night.

If you want a more rural and genuine atmosphere, rent a villa on Nevis. Some of the greatest villas on Nevis are:

The Lighthouse: A four-star property on the west coast of Nevis near Pinney's Beach. It contains three bedrooms with en-suite bathrooms, a living room, a dining room, a kitchen, a laundry room, a terrace, a pool, a jacuzzi, a grilling area, and free Wi-Fi. The charges start at $500 per night.

The Hermitage Plantation Inn: A three-star villa in the center portion of Nevis near Gingerland. It features 15 rooms and cottages with air conditioning, TVs with cable channels, telephones, bathrooms with hairdryers, verandas overlooking the garden or the mountains, a pool, a restaurant, a bar, and free Wi-Fi. The costs start at $200 per night.

Golden Rock Inn: A three-star villa on the east coast of Nevis near Windward Side. It features 11 rooms and cottages with air conditioning, TVs with DVD players, telephones, bathrooms with hairdryers, patios overlooking the garden or the ocean, a pool, a restaurant, a bar, and free Wi-Fi. The prices start at $175 per night.

How to Get There

The simplest method to go to St. Kitts and Nevis is via aircraft. Direct flights are from the US, Canada, UK, and other Caribbean islands to Robert L. Bradshaw International Airport on St. Kitts and Vance W. Amory International Airport on Nevis. You may also take a ferry or a water taxi between the two islands, which takes around 45 minutes.

To get to the hotels, resorts, and villas, you will need to arrange a cab or a shuttle service that offers transportation from the airport or the ferry terminal to your Accommodation. You may also hire a vehicle or a bike if you wish to explore the islands on your own.

Prices

The rates for lodging in St. Kitts and Nevis vary based on the season, the location, the kind, and the quality of your hotel. Generally speaking, you may expect to spend roughly

$100 for a budget hotel or villa, $200 for a mid-range hotel or resort, $300 for a luxury hotel or resort, and $500 for a premium villa each night.

These prices normally include taxes and fees. However, some motels may charge extra for breakfast, parking, internet access, etc. You may also choose to tip your personnel if you are delighted with their service.

Hotels, resorts, and villas are some of the lodging choices you may pick from when visiting St. Kitts and Nevis. Depending on your budget and inclination, you may discover a location that meets your taste and demands. You may enjoy the beach, the golf course, the casino, the nightlife, the colonial elegance, the botanical gardens, and the local cuisine on both islands.

The budget, mid-range, and Luxury alternatives

St. Kitts and Nevis is a twin-island country in the Caribbean that provides a range of experiences for people of varied budgets and inclinations. Whether searching for a calm beach escape, a cultural immersion, or an adventure-filled holiday, you will find something to fit your taste and pocketbook in this delightful region. Here are some top alternatives for budget, mid-range, and luxury tourists in St. Kitts & Nevis.

Budget If you are traveling on a low budget, you may still experience the beauty and variety of St. Kitts and Nevis without breaking the bank. Numerous inexpensive lodgings, sights, and activities will offer you a flavor of the local culture and environment.

Stay at the Culture House1, a charming guesthouse that provides dormitories and private rooms with communal bathrooms, beginning at $25 per night. The Culture House is in Basseterre, the capital of St. Kitts. It is within walking distance of various historical and cultural monuments, such as the National Museum2, the Independence Square3, and the Berkeley Memorial. The Culture House also offers trips

157

and activities for visitors, such as trekking, snorkeling, drumming, and culinary lessons. The Culture House is open from 8:00 a.m. to 10:00 p.m. every day. You may take a cab from the airport for around $15 USD or a public bus for about $1 USD to get there.

Visit the Brimstone Hill Fortress National Park, a UNESCO World Heritage Site that displays the history and architecture of St. Kitts. The British erected the stronghold in the 17th and 18th centuries to protect the island against French invasions and provide beautiful views of the Caribbean Sea and the adjacent islands. You may visit the fortifications, barracks, cannons, museum, and gardens for $10 per adult and $5 per kid. The park is open from 9:30 a.m. until 5:30 p.m. every day. You may take a cab for around $20 USD or a public bus for about $2 USD to get there.

Enjoy the natural splendor of St. Kitts by trekking the Mount Liamuiga Volcano, the highest point on the island at 3,792 feet (1,156 meters). The journey takes between 4 to 6 hours roundway, depending on your fitness level and speed, and travels through beautiful jungle, farmland, and rocky terrain. Reward yourself with panoramic views of the island and the crater lake at the peak. The trek is tough and needs a guide, which you can arrange via your hostel or a local tour operator for approximately $50 per person, including transportation and lunch.

Mid-range: If you have a moderate budget and want to enjoy more comfort and convenience in St. Kitts and Nevis, you may select from various alternatives that provide additional facilities and services without breaking the bank.

Stay at the Ocean Terrace Inn, a four-star hotel with large rooms and suites with balconies overlooking the ocean or the garden, beginning at $150 per night. The hotel is situated in Portland, a calm area in Basseterre, and is near various attractions, such as the St. Kitts Scenic Railway, the Royal St. Kitts Golf Club, and the Frigate Bay Beach. The hotel also has a shuttle service, two restaurants, a bar, an outdoor pool, a fitness center, and a spa. The Ocean Terrace Inn is open 24 hours a day. To get there, you may take a cab from the airport for around $20 or organize a ride with the hotel for about $25.

Visit the Nevis Botanical Gardens, a tropical wonderland that highlights the flora and wildlife of Nevis and other places around the globe. The gardens stretch over 7 acres (2.8 hectares) and contain numerous themed sections, such as the orchid house, the cactus garden, the rainforest conservatory, and the herb garden. You may also enjoy statues, fountains, ponds, and bridges throughout the grounds. The admission cost is $13 USD per adult and $8 USD per kid. The gardens are open from 9:00 a.m. to 4:00 p.m. Monday through Saturday. To reach there, you can take a boat from Basseterre to Charlestown for around $5, then take a cab for about $10, or hire a vehicle for about $40 per day.

Enjoy the culinary pleasures of St. Kitts and Nevis by eating at the Spice Mill Restaurant, a seaside restaurant that provides local and international food with a twist. The restaurant is situated on Cockleshell Bay, a picturesque beach on the southern coast of St. Kitts, and provides spectacular views of Nevis and the sunset. You may relish meals like lobster thermidor, jerk chicken, coconut curry, grilled mahi-mahi, drinks, wines, and desserts. The average price for a supper is roughly $40 USD per person. The restaurant is open from 11:00 a.m. to 10:00 p.m. from Tuesday to Sunday. You may take a cab for approximately $30 or hire a vehicle for about $40 daily to get there.

Luxury If you have a liberal budget and want to enjoy the greatest that St. Kitts & Nevis offers, you may spend on alternatives that provide the pinnacle in luxury and exclusivity.

Stay at the Park Hyatt St. Kitts, a five-star resort providing beautiful rooms and suites with balconies or terraces, some with plunge pools or outdoor showers, beginning at $500 per night. The resort is situated on Banana Bay, a quiet beach on the southeast coast of St. Kitts, and provides beautiful views of Nevis and the ocean. The resort also has three restaurants, two bars, two pools, a spa, a fitness center, a kids' club, and a golf course. The Park Hyatt St. Kitts is open 24 hours a day. You may take a cab from the airport for around $40 or organize a ride with the resort for about $50 to get there.

Visit the Four Seasons Resort Nevis, a five-star resort that provides magnificent rooms and suites with balconies or patios, some with private pools or hot tubs, beginning at $600 USD per night. The resort is situated on Pinney's Beach, a beautiful beach on the west coast of Nevis, and provides excellent views of St. Kitts and the sunset. The resort also has four restaurants, three bars, three pools, a spa, a fitness center, a tennis court, and a golf course. The Four Seasons Resort Nevis is open 24 hours a day. To get there, you may take a boat from Basseterre to Charlestown for around $5 USD, then take a cab for about $15 USD, or organize a shuttle with the resort for about $20 USD.

Enjoy the ultimate thrill in St. Kitts and Nevis by soaring with Sky Safari trips, a firm that provides ziplining trips above the rainforest canopy and the Wingfield River. The trips are ideal for all ages and fitness levels, including safety equipment, instruction, transportation, and refreshments. You may pick from four trips, ranging from $89 to $129 per person, depending on the quantity and length of zip lines. The tours range from 2 to 3 hours and are accessible from 8:30 a.m. to 3:30 p.m. daily. You may contact Sky Safari Tours online or by phone to arrange your trip.

The cheap, mid-range, and luxury alternatives are some of the ways to experience St. Kitts & Nevis according to your tastes and resources. Whether you are searching for a low-cost, comfortable, or lavish holiday, you will undoubtedly find something to meet your requirements and expectations in this twin-island country.

The local, regional, and international cuisines

Here are some of the greatest restaurants to eat on St. Kitts and Nevis, along with some recommendations on how to get there, when to go, and where to stay.

Local Cuisine

St. Kitts and Nevis have a significant culinary tradition reflecting African, European, and Indian influences. Some of the local delicacies include goat water, a hearty stew made with goat meat, breadfruit, and dumplings; stewed saltfish, the national meal of salted cod cooked with coconut milk, vegetables, and spices; and black pudding, a savory sausage prepared with hog blood and rice. You may also taste some tropical fruits that thrive on the islands, such as mangoes, papayas, guavas, soursops, and sugar apples.

One of the greatest venues to enjoy local food is El Fredo's Restaurant and Bar, in Basseterre, St. Kitts's capital. This family-owned restaurant delivers classic Kittitian meals in a comfortable and welcoming ambiance. You may taste conch soup, lobster thermidor, jerk chicken, and coconut cake. The restaurant is open from Monday to Saturday from 11:30

a.m. to 10 p.m. and Sunday from 12 p.m. to 9 p.m. The rates vary from $10 to $30 USD per person.

To get to El Fredo's Restaurant and Bar from the airport, you can take a cab for around $15 or a bus for about $1. The restaurant is situated on Bay Road, near the ferry station. If you are searching for a place to stay nearby, you may check out the Bird Rock Beach Hotel, a three-star hotel that provides pleasant rooms with gardens, pool, or ocean views. The hotel also features an outdoor pool, a garden, and a communal lounge. The prices start at $95 each night.

Regional Cuisine

St. Kitts and Nevis are part of the Caribbean area, noted for its bright and rich food. You may get recipes from various Caribbean islands, such as Jamaica, Trinidad, Barbados, and Cuba, as well as fusion dishes that merge Caribbean components with other cuisines. Some of the traditional foods that you may try include roti, a flatbread loaded with meat or vegetables; jerk pig or chicken, marinated in a spicy sauce and grilled; conch fritters, deep-fried balls of conch flesh and batter; and rum cake, a moist cake steeped in rum syrup.

One of the greatest venues to experience native food is Spice Mill Restaurant, situated on Cockleshell Bay in St. Kitts. This beachside eatery offers stunning views of the neighboring island of Nevis and the Caribbean Sea. You may taste curry goat roti, jerk lobster spaghetti, conch ceviche, and rum raisin cheesecake. The restaurant is open Tuesday through Sunday from 11:30 a.m. to 10 p.m. and Monday from 5 p.m. to 10 p.m. The rates vary from $15 to $45 per person.

To get to Spice Mill Restaurant from Basseterre, you may take a cab for around $25 USD or a bus for about $2 USD. The restaurant is situated at the end of Cockleshell Bay Road. If you are searching for a place to stay nearby, you may check out the Park Hyatt St. Kitts Christophe Harbour, a five-star resort with exquisite villas with balconies, Jacuzzi tubs, and garden or ocean views. The resort also contains three swimming pools, a spa, a golf course, and four restaurants. The charges start at $750 USD per night.

International Cuisine

St. Kitts and Nevis are not just impacted by their Caribbean neighbors but also by their past colonial powers and their international links. You can discover cuisines from throughout the globe on these islands, such as Indian, Chinese, Italian, French, American, and British. Some foreign foods you should try include chicken tikka masala, fried rice with shrimp or chicken, pizza Margherita, escargots, burgers, and fish and chips.

One of the best venues to experience foreign food is Marshalls near Frigate Bay in St. Kitts. This beautiful poolside restaurant combines Caribbean and foreign cuisines, with delicacies such as coconut shrimp, lamb chops, escargots, and lobster thermidor. A library bar and a wide range of wines are also available at the restaurant. The restaurant is open Monday to Saturday from 6 p.m. to 10 p.m. and Sunday from 11 a.m. to 3 p.m. for brunch. The rates vary from $25 to $65 per person.

To get to Marshalls from Basseterre, you can take a cab for around $10 or a bus for about $1. The restaurant is on Zenway Boulevard, near the Royal St. Kitts Golf Club. If you are searching for a place to stay nearby, you may check out the Royal St. Kitts Hotel, a four-star hotel with contemporary rooms with balconies, kitchenettes, and garden or ocean views. The hotel also offers an outdoor pool, a fitness center, and a garden. The prices start at $179 per night.

Summary

St. Kitts and Nevis are islands that provide a rich and varied gastronomic experience for vacationers. You may discover local, regional, and international cuisines on these islands, with dishes that reflect their African, European, and Indian origins and their Caribbean characteristics. Some of the greatest places to dine on St. Kitts and Nevis include El Fredo's Restaurant and Bar, Spice Mill Restaurant, Marshalls, and many more.

The best locations to dine, drink, and party

St. Kitts and Nevis may be small in size, but they are huge in taste. The twin-island country provides various eating alternatives, from informal beach bars to upscale restaurants, providing local and foreign food. Whether you seek fresh seafood, spicy curries, or delicious sweets, you will find something to delight your taste buds in St. Kitts and Nevis. Here are some top spots to dine, drink, and party in this Caribbean paradise.

Tiranga

If you enjoy Indian cuisine, you can't miss Tiranga, a quaint and traditional restaurant in Frigate Bay, St. Kitts. The menu contains a selection of cuisines from various parts of India, such as samosas, biryanis, tandoori meats, and curries. The naan bread is freshly cooked, and the raita is handmade. The servings are large, and the pricing is fair. If you ask the courteous staff, you may even request off-menu delicacies, such as fish curry or lamb rogan josh. Tiranga is open for lunch and supper from Monday through Saturday and for dinner only on Sunday. It is at Frigate Bay Road, near the Royal St. Kitts Hotel. You may take a cab or bus from Basseterre to reach there.

Address: Frigate Bay Road, Frigate Bay, St. Kitts Opening hours: Mon-Sat 11:30 a.m.-2:30 p.m. and 6 p.m.-10 p.m.; Sun 6 p.m.-10 p.m. Prices: Main meals from $15 Closest hotel/accommodation: Royal St. Kitts Hotel (4 stars, from $200 per night)

Bananas

For a romantic and gorgeous dining experience, visit Bananas, a hilltop restaurant at Hamilton Estate, Nevis. Lovely grounds surrounds the restaurant and provide wonderful ocean views. The menu comprises Caribbean and international cuisine, including lobster salad, blackened grouper, panko fried brie, and coconut shrimp. The desserts are particularly fantastic, notably the chocolate cake and the banana split. Bananas are available for supper from Tuesday through Sunday and lunch on Sunday. It is situated at Hamilton Estate Road, approximately 15 minutes from Charlestown. You may book a table online or by phone.

Address: Hamilton Estate Road, Hamilton Estate, Nevis Opening hours: Tue-Sat 6 p.m.-9:30 p.m.; Sun 12 p.m.-3 p.m. and 6 p.m.-9:30 p.m. Prices: Main meals from $25

Closest hotel/accommodation: Montpelier Plantation & Beach (4 stars, from $300 per night)

Drink

Shipwreck Beach Bar & Grill

If you are searching for a laid-back and pleasant location to drink by the beach, go no further than Shipwreck Beach Bar and Grill in South Friars Bay, St. Kitts. This renowned place draws residents and visitors alike with its rustic appeal and vibrant atmosphere. You may sip on a refreshing Carib beer or a rum punch while listening to live music or watching sports on the big screen. The culinary selection provides delectable snacks and meals, such as fish tacos, jerk chicken, ribs, burgers, and salads. Shipwreck Beach Bar and Grill is open daily from 10 a.m. to 10 p.m. It is situated at South Friars Bay Road, approximately 10 minutes from Basseterre.

Address: South Friars Bay Road, South Friars Bay, St. Kitts Opening hours: Daily 10 a.m.-10 p.m. Prices: Drinks from $3; Food from $10 Closest hotel/accommodation: Park Hyatt St. Kitts Christophe Harbour (5 stars, from $500 per night)

Sunshine's Beach Bar & Grill

One of the most renowned beach bars in the Caribbean is Sunshine's Beach Bar & Grill on Pinney's Beach, Nevis. This bright and comfortable establishment is famed for its trademark cocktail, the Killer Bee, a strong mix of rum, honey, passion fruit juice, and hidden ingredients. Be cautious not to drink too many of them, or you could buzz like a bee. The cuisine comprises Caribbean favorites, such as conch fritters, BBQ chicken breast, grilled mahi mahi, and lobster. Sunshine's Beach Bar & Grill is open from 11 a.m. to 11 p.m. It is near Pinney's Beach Road, adjacent to the Four Seasons Resort.

Address: Pinney's Beach Road, Pinney's Beach, Nevis Opening hours: Daily 11 a.m.-11 p.m. Prices: Drinks from $5; Food from $15 Closest hotel/accommodation: Four Seasons Resort Nevis ([5 stars], from $600 per night)

Party

Spice Mill Restaurant

If you want to dance the night away beneath the stars, Spice Mill Restaurant in Cockleshell Bay, St. Kitts, is the place to be. This elegant and contemporary restaurant evolves into a vibrant nightclub on Saturday evenings, with DJs playing the latest tunes and a full-service bar. You may also have a great supper before hitting the dance floor, with specialties such as Thai chicken strips, conch fritters, lobster spaghetti, and steak. Spice Mill Restaurant is open for lunch and supper from Tuesday to Sunday and for brunch on Sunday. It is situated at Cockleshell Bay Road, approximately a 20-minute drive from Basseterre.

Address: Cockleshell Bay Road, Cockleshell Bay, St. Kitts Opening hours: Tue-Sat 12 p.m.-10 p.m.; Sun 10 a.m.-10 p.m. Prices: Drinks from $5; Food from $20 Closest hotel/accommodation: Park Hyatt St. Kitts Christophe Harbour (5 stars, from $500 per night)

The Gin Trap

If you love gin, you will appreciate The Gin Trap, a sleek and quiet pub in Jones Bay, Nevis. The bar showcases over 100 kinds of gin from across the globe and other spirits, wines, beers, and cocktails. You may also try some of the local gins, such as Clifton Estate or Nevisian Spirit. The food selection comprises snacks and meals, such as cheese boards, burgers, pizzas, and salads. The Gin Trap is open every day from 12 p.m. until 10 p.m. It is situated at Jones Bay Road, approximately 10 minutes from Charlestown.

Address: Jones Bay Road, Jones Bay, Nevis Opening hours: Daily 12 p.m.-10 p.m. Prices: Drinks from $4; Food from $10 Closest hotel/accommodation: Nisbet Plantation Beach Club ([4 stars], from $250 per night)

The best places to eat, drink, and party in St. Kitts and Nevis are only a taste of the numerous alternatives available for those who wish to enjoy the culture and cuisine of this Caribbean island. Whether you like informal or sophisticated eating, local or foreign cuisines, peaceful or bustling settings, you will find something to fit your mood and taste in St. Kitts and Nevis. You may also explore these islands' history, wildlife, and attractions during the day and enjoy the nightlife and entertainment at night. St. Kitts and Nevis is a place that provides something for everyone.

CHAPTER 6

3-7 Days Itinerary

St. Kitts and Nevis, a twin-island republic in the Caribbean that uniquely combines natural beauty, rich history, and dynamic culture. Whether searching for a quiet beach break, an exciting outdoor experience, or a cultural immersion, you will find something to fit your taste and budget in this tropical paradise. Here is a proposed schedule for 3-7 days in St. Kitts and Nevis, including the greatest sites, activities, and food on both islands.

Day 1

Explore Basseterre and Frigate Bay. Start your journey in St. Kitts' capital city, Basseterre, where you can appreciate the colonial architecture, see the National Museum, and browse for local goods at the Amina Craft Market1. For lunch, travel to El Fredo's, a famous venue for real Kittitian food, such as stewed saltfish, goat water, and souse. Try their unique rum punch, crafted with fresh and local fruit juices.

In the afternoon, take a short drive or taxi ride to Frigate Bay, a gorgeous region with two beaches: one on the Atlantic and one on the Caribbean. The Atlantic side is excellent for surfing and windsurfing, while the Caribbean is quieter and perfect for swimming and snorkeling. You may also enjoy a game of golf at the Royal St. Kitts Golf Club, which provides beautiful views of both seas.

For supper, select from one of the numerous restaurants and bars along "The Strip," a busy strip of beach on the Caribbean side of Frigate Bay. You may find anything from simple beach shacks to gourmet dining venues providing local and foreign delicacies. Some popular venues include Mr. X's Shiggidy Shack, Boozies on the Beach, and Spice Mill. After supper, join the party at The Strip, where you can dance to live music, view fire performances, and socialize with locals and visitors alike.

Day 2

Discover Brimstone Hill Fortress and Romney Manor. Today, you will see some of the historical and cultural landmarks of St. Kitts. Start with a visit to Brimstone Hill Fortress, a UNESCO World Heritage Site erected by the British in the 17th and 18th centuries. The stronghold is built on a hill overlooking the sea, giving panoramic views of the island and nearby islands. You may visit the walls, barracks, cannons, and museum and learn about the history of St. Kitts and its participation in the colonial conflicts.

Drive to Romney Manor, a historic sugar estate now occupied by Caribelle Batik, a regional handicraft company that creates colorful fabrics using a time-honored wax-resist method. You may observe the craftspeople at work, browse for souvenirs, and wander around the gorgeous grounds surrounding the house. Don't miss the 400-year-old saman tree that shadows the lawn, which is claimed to be one of the biggest in the world.

For lunch, stop into Sprat Net, a rustic seafood restaurant that is set on a fishing beach near Old Road Town. You may taste fresh fish, lobster, conch, and other delicacies grilled over an open fire, along with sides like rice and peas, plantains, and coleslaw. The restaurant is open exclusively on Wednesdays and Fridays from 12 p.m. until 10 p.m.

In the afternoon, you may either relax on one of the local beaches, such as Cockleshell Bay or Banana Bay or take an extra journey up Mount Liamuiga, the highest point on St. Kitts. The journey entails a difficult climb through the jungle to the crater rim of the dormant volcano, where you can enjoy breathtaking views of the island and beyond. The excursion takes roughly 5 hours round-trip and costs $75 per person.

For the evening, drive back to Basseterre and try one of the restaurants at Port Zante, a contemporary waterfront complex that offers stores, cafés, art galleries, and entertainment venues. Some of the recommended places are Ballahoo, which serves Caribbean and international cuisine with a view of The Circus (a roundabout modeled after Piccadilly Circus in London), Serendipity, which offers fine dining in an elegant setting overlooking the harbor, and Rituals Sushi, which specializes in fresh sushi and sashimi.

Day 3

Take a catamaran voyage to Nevis. Today, you will visit St. Kitts' sister island, Nevis, which is only a short boat or catamaran ride away. You may take a public boat from

Basseterre to Charlestown (the capital of Nevis) for $10 round-trip or charter a catamaran excursion that includes snorkeling, lunch, and cocktails for $125 per person. The catamaran excursion starts from Port Zante at 9 a.m., returns at 4 p.m., and stops at a hidden bay where you may snorkel amid coral reefs and exotic fish. You will also have time to visit Charlestown, a picturesque town with colonial buildings, museums, and shops.

Once you arrive in Nevis, you may take a guided tour of the island or explore independently. Some of the highlights of Nevis are:

The Botanical Gardens of Nevis include a variety of plants, flowers, and sculptures from across the globe, as well as a reproduction of a Thai home and a restaurant that offers Thai food.

The Museum of Nevis History is situated in the birthplace of Alexander Hamilton, one of the United States' founding fathers. The museum includes exhibits and memorabilia linked to Hamilton's life and legacy, as well as the history and culture of Nevis.

The Nevis Peak Trail is a hard walk to the peak of Nevis Peak, the highest point on the island. The terrain is steep and treacherous and needs a guide and suitable equipment. The climb takes around 4 hours round-trip and costs $100 per person.

Pinney's beach is one of the most popular beaches on Nevis, with smooth white sand, brilliant blue sea, and palm palms. You may relax on the beach, swim, or hire water sports equipment. You may also visit the Four Seasons Resort, which is situated on the beach and provides luxury facilities, such as a golf course, a spa, and various restaurants and bars.

For lunch, you may either dine at one of the restaurants or beach bars on Pinney's Beach, such as Sunshine's, famed for its Killer Bee cocktail and grilled lobster, or Lime Beach Bar, which provides fresh seafood and pizza. Alternatively, you may try one of the local cafes in Charlestown, such as Mem's Pizzaria, which provides great pizza and pasta dishes, or Rodney's Cuisine, which serves traditional Nevisian cuisine, such as stewed goat, jerk chicken, and johnnycakes.

For supper, you may either return to St. Kitts by boat or catamaran or remain overnight on Nevis if you have more time. There are several housing choices on Nevis, ranging from inexpensive guesthouses to luxury resorts. Some of the suggested locations are:

The Hermitage Plantation Inn is a historic plantation mansion turned into a pleasant inn with 15 cottages. The inn features a restaurant that provides Caribbean and international cuisine with local ingredients, a bar that offers rum tastings and live music, and a pool that overlooks the grounds. The prices start at $200 per night.

The Montpelier Plantation & Beach is a boutique hotel built on a historic sugar plantation with 19 rooms and suites. The hotel boasts a private beach club that provides:

- Free shuttle service.
- A spa that offers massages and treatments.
- Three restaurants that serve gourmet food with organic ingredients.
- The prices start at $300 USD per night.

The Golden Rock Inn is a sophisticated hotel located on the slopes of Nevis Peak with 11 rooms and cottages. The hotel boasts a restaurant that provides inventive meals with local tastes, a bar showcasing specialty drinks and wines, and a pool with spectacular views of the island and the sea. The prices start at $250 per night.

Day 4

Enjoy a beautiful train excursion and zip-lining adventure. If you stay for more than 3 days in St. Kitts and Nevis, you may use this day to enjoy some of the great things the islands offer. One of these is the St. Kitts Scenic Railway, a 3-hour trip that takes you across the island on a narrow-gauge train previously used to carry sugar cane. The trip allows you to observe the landscape, the shoreline, and the communities of St. Kitts from a fresh perspective. You may also enjoy free beverages, food on board, live commentary, and music. The excursion costs $129 per person and leaves from Needsmust Station at 8:30 a.m. or 12:30 p.m.

Another activity you may attempt is zip-lining at Sky Safari Tours, which is near Wingfield Estate in Old Road Town. You may select from four distinct zip lines that vary from 250 feet to 1,350 feet in length and fly over the rainforest canopy at speeds up to 50 miles per hour. You may also enjoy views of the Brimstone Hill Fortress, the Caribbean Sea, and the nearby islands. The zip-lining excursion costs $89 per person and lasts for 2 hours. You may pick from numerous periods between 8 a.m. and 3 p.m.

Either go to Ottley's Plantation Inn, a luxury hotel and a regional restaurant, serving Caribbean dishes like roti, curry, and jerk chicken.

In the afternoon, you may either rest at your hotel or beach or take another optional excursion to the Black Rocks, which are volcanic structures that are situated on the northeastern coast of St. Kitts. You may observe the contrast between the black rocks and the blue ocean and snap some shots of the spectacular environment. You may also explore the adjacent Dieppe Bay settlement, the oldest settlement on St. Kitts, which boasts a black sand beach, a fort, and a church.

For supper, you may either return to your hotel or try one of the restaurants in Basseterre or Frigate Bay that you have not visited yet.

Day 5

Go snorkeling or diving at Booby Island or Monkey Shoals. If you stay for more than 4 days in St. Kitts and Nevis, you may spend this day exploring some of the underwater marvels the islands offer. You may either go snorkeling or diving at Booby Island or Monkey Shoals, which are two of the top spots for marine life and coral reefs in the vicinity.

Booby Island is a tiny island approximately 2 miles off the coast of St. Kitts and is home to a huge colony of brown boobies (a seabird species). The island is bordered by beautiful water and colorful coral reefs that contain a variety of fish, turtles, rays, and sharks. You may take a boat tour from Basseterre or Frigate Bay with snorkeling or diving equipment, lunch, and beverages for $85 per person, or rent your equipment and take a water taxi from White House Bay for $20 per person.

Monkey Shoals is a group of coral reefs situated approximately 4 miles off Nevis's coast and accessible by boat from Charlestown or Pinney's Beach. The reefs are filled with marine life, such as angelfish, butterflyfish, parrotfish, barracuda, grouper, and lobster. You may also glimpse dolphins, turtles, and even whales in the deeper sea. You can either book a snorkeling or diving tour with one of the local operators, such as Scuba Safaris or Nevis Dive Centre, that includes equipment, lunch, and drinks for $100 USD per person or rent your own equipment and join a boat trip from one of the hotels or beach bars on Pinney's Beach for $50 USD per person.

For lunch, you may either dine on board the boat or on one of the beaches on Booby Island or Nevis. You may even bring your picnic if you wish.

In the afternoon, you may either continue snorkeling or diving at Booby Island or Monkey Shoals or return to your hotel or beach and rest.

For supper, you may either dine at your hotel or try one of the restaurants on St. Kitts or Nevis that you have not visited yet.

Day 6

Enjoy a day excursion to St. Eustatius or Saba. If you stay for more than 5 days in St. Kitts and Nevis, you may use this day to explore one of the nearby islands of St. Eustatius or Saba, which are part of the Dutch Caribbean. Both islands are noted for their natural beauty and solitude and provide a distinct experience from St. Kitts and Nevis.

St. Eustatius (also known as Statia) is a tiny island approximately 10 miles south of St. Kitts and has a rich history as a former commerce center in the 18th century. You may tour the remains of Fort Oranje, which was once the hub of trade and defense on the island, visit the Historical Museum, which showcases relics and exhibits linked to Statia's past, and buy local products at the Old Gin House. You may also trek to the summit of The Quill, an extinct volcano that has a lush rainforest within its crater, swim or dive at one of the numerous spots around the island that offer wrecks, coral reefs, and marine life, or relax on one of the calm beaches, such as Zeelandia Beach or Oranje Bay Beach.

Saba is a tiny island approximately 20 miles southwest of St. Kitts and boasts a rough scenery with high cliffs and rocky shorelines. One can embark on a hike to the peak of Mount Scenery, which stands as the highest point in the Dutch Caribbean, and relish in the awe-inspiring views of the island and the surrounding sea. Additionally, a visit to the Saba Museum presents a great opportunity to learn about the history and culture of Saba and its people. Lastly, shopping for local handicrafts is made possible at the Saba Lace Shop or the Saba Artisan Foundation. You may also snorkel or dive at one of the spots surrounding the island that showcase pinnacles, caves, and volcanic formations or sunbathe on one of the hidden coves, such as Wells Bay or Cove Bay.

You may either plan a day trip to St. Eustatius or Saba with one of the local operators, such as Blue Water Safaris or Winair, that includes round-way flights, transfers, and excursions for $200 USD per person or organize your own flights and tours with the airlines and guides on the islands. The flights take around 20 minutes each way and leave from Robert L. Bradshaw International Airport in St. Kitts.

For lunch, you may either dine at one of the restaurants or cafés on St. Eustatius or Saba, such as The Old Gin House, which provides world cuisine with a Caribbean flare on Statia, or Brigadoon, which offers seafood and steak meals with a view of the port on Saba. Alternatively, you may bring your picnic if you wish.

In the afternoon, you may either continue touring St. Eustatius or Saba or return to St. Kitts and rest.

For supper, you may either dine at your hotel or try one of the restaurants on St. Kitts that you have not visited yet.

Day 7

Rest and leave. If you stay for more than 6 days in St. Kitts and Nevis, you may spend this day resting and enjoying your final moments on the islands. You may spend some time on your favorite beach or hotel pool or do some last-minute shopping or sightseeing in Basseterre or

Charlestown. You may also treat yourself to a spa session or a massage at one of the hotels or wellness centers on the islands, such as The Spa at Four Seasons Resort Nevis or Emerald Mist Spa at St. Kitts Marriott Resort.

For lunch, you may either dine at your hotel or try one of the restaurants you have not visited yet on St. Kitts or Nevis.
You must pack your luggage in the afternoon and check out from your hotel. Depending on your flight itinerary, you must take a boat or catamaran from Nevis to St. Kitts if you are staying on Nevis and then take a cab or shuttle to Robert L. Bradshaw International Airport on St. Kitts. You should arrive at the airport at least 2 hours prior to your flight's departure time to complete immigration and security procedures.

You have reached the end of the 3-7 Days Itinerary chapter for St. Kitts and Nevis. In this chapter, we have provided you a proposed itinerary for your vacation to this beautiful twin-island country, encompassing the major sites, activities, and food on both islands and some of the adjacent islands you may visit as day excursions. However, this is not the only way to experience St. Kitts and Nevis; you are free to personalize your vacation according to your interests and tastes. You may also check out the other chapters in this travel guide for additional insights and suggestions on St. Kitts and Nevis, such as the history, culture, climate, transportation, safety, and more.

CHAPTER 7

Resources and Contacts

St. Kitts and Nevis offers a wide range of resources to help you plan and make the most of your vacation. Whether you need to learn more about visa requirements, health and safety measures, currency and exchange rates, or transportation and communication alternatives, you will discover several official and credible sites to help you. One of the benefits of visiting St. Kitts and Nevis is that it is simple to reach since it has direct flights from numerous major cities in North America and Europe and regional links from other Caribbean islands.

You can also pick from several kinds of lodging, such as hotels, resorts, villas, or guest homes, based on your budget, comfort, and desire. Each kind of housing has unique characteristics and amenities, so you can determine what works best for you. In this travel guidebook, we will introduce you to the numerous resources and contacts accessible in St. Kitts and Nevis, and offer you some suggestions and advice on how to utilize them. We will also supply you with some information on what to anticipate and prepare for your trip and some advice on how to make your travel arrangements. We hope that this book will assist you in having a smooth and pleasurable journey to St. Kitts & Nevis.

The immigration and Visa requirements

St. Kitts and Nevis is a location that invites people from all over the globe to experience its natural beauty, cultural variety, and historical charm. However, before you pack your bags and book your flight, you must know basic immigration and visa requirements and a list of visa-exempted nations for St. Kitts and Nevis.

Immigration requirements

To enter St. Kitts and Nevis, you must have a valid passport for at least six months from arrival. You also need a return or onward ticket, evidence of adequate finances, and proof of lodging. You may be requested to present these papers at the port of entry by the immigration agents. You must also complete immigration and customs declaration forms, which will be supplied on the aircraft or at the airport. You need to retain these forms with you until you leave the country.

Visa requirements

The visa requirements for St. Kitts and Nevis vary on your nationality, reason of travel, and length of stay. St. Kitts and

Nevis have three visa regimes: visa-free, visa-on-arrival, and visa-required.

Visa-free: If you are a citizen of one of the 104 visa-exempt countries, you may visit St. Kitts and Nevis as a tourist without a visa for stays up to the time specified below:

6 months: Bahamas, Barbados, Belize, Canada, Guyana, Jamaica, Suriname, Trinidad and Tobago, United States

3 months: All EU citizens, Albania, Argentina, Australia, Bahrain, Bangladesh, Bolivia, Botswana, Brazil, Brunei, Chile, China, Colombia, Costa Rica, Ecuador, Egypt, El Salvador, Eswatini, Fiji, Gambia, Ghana, Guatemala, Honduras, Hong Kong, Iceland, India, Israel, Japan, Jordan, Kenya, Kiribati, Kuwait, Lesotho, Liechtenstein, Malawi, Malaysia, Maldives, Malta, Mauritius, Mexico, Moldova, Monaco, Nauru, New Zealand, Nicaragua, Nigeria, North Macedonia, Norway, Panama, Papua New Guinea, Paraguay, Peru, Qatar, Russia, Rwanda, San Marino, Saudi Arabia, Serbia, Seychelles, Sierra Leone, Singapore, Solomon Islands, South Africa, South Korea, Sri Lanka, Switzerland, Taiwan, Tanzania, Tonga, Turkey, Tuvalu, Uganda, Ukraine, United Arab Emirates, United

Kingdom (including BOTC passport holders of Montserrat), Uruguay Vanuatu Vatican City Venezuela Zambia Zimbabwe

30 days: Belarus, Indonesia, Macau

27 days: Cuba

Visa-on-arrival: If you are a citizen of one of the following countries or territories that are not mentioned above as visa-exempt or visa-required (see below), you may receive a visa on arrival at the port of entry for a charge of US$100. The visa is valid for up to 30 days and may be renewed for another 30 days at the immigration office in Basseterre or Charlestown.

Visa-required: If you are a citizen of one of the following countries or territories that are not mentioned above as visa-exempt or visa-on-arrival (see above), you need to apply for a visa in advance at the closest St. Kitts and Nevis diplomatic mission or consulate before your travel. The visa application process may vary by country. You may need to provide documents such as your passport (valid for at least six months from the date of your arrival), passport photos (two or four depending on the country), completed application form (available online or at the embassy/consulate), proof of travel itinerary (flight reservation and hotel booking), proof of financial means (bank statement or letter from employer/sponsor), proof of purpose of visit (invitation letter or confirmation letter from host/organization), police clearance certificate (if required by the embassy/consulate), and visa fee (US$100). The processing period may take two weeks to two months, depending on the nation where you apply.

Afghanistan, Algeria, Angola, Benin, Bhutan, Burkina Faso, Burundi, Cambodia, Cameroon, Cape Verde, Central African Republic, Chad, Comoros Congo (Democratic Republic) Congo (Republic) Côte d'Ivoire Djibouti Dominican Republic Equatorial Guinea Eritrea Ethiopia Gabon Guinea Guinea-Bissau Haiti (except holders of diplomatic or official passports or normal passports traveling on business) Iran Iraq Kazakhstan Kyrgyzstan Laos Lebanon Liberia Libya Madagascar Mali Mauritania Mongolia Mozambique Myanmar Namibia Nepal Niger Pakistan Palestine Philippines Samoa (Western) São Tomé and Príncipe Senegal Somalia Syria Tajikistan Timor-Leste (East Timor) Turkmenistan Uzbekistan Vietnam Yemen

St. Kitts and Nevis is a place that provides a lot of fun and adventure for those who are searching for a distinctive Caribbean experience. By knowing some basic information about immigration and visa requirements and a list of visa-exempted nations for St. Kitts and Nevis, you can prepare yourself for a smooth and pleasurable vacation that will leave you with memorable memories.

The currency, language, and climatic information

St. Kitts and Nevis is a location that combines natural beauty, cultural variety, and historical charm. It is vital to have some basic knowledge about the island federation's currency, language, and environment to make the most of your vacation.

Currency

The official currency of St. Kitts and Nevis is the Eastern Caribbean Dollar (XCD), which has a fixed exchange rate of 2.7 XCD to 1 USD. You may convert your foreign money at banks, hotels, or authorized dealers, but be aware of the costs and exchange rates that may vary. Most shops will take US Dollars as a means of payment, but never coins — change will always be offered in XCD.

At most establishments, you may also use major credit cards, such as Visa, MasterCard, and American Express, although some may charge a service fee or demand a minimum transaction. ATMs are generally accessible in St. Kitts and Nevis, although they may charge a withdrawal fee or restrict the amount you withdraw each day. Having some cash with you for little purchases, gratuities, or emergencies is good.

Language

The official language spoken in St. Kitts and Nevis is English. However, suppose you have never visited the Caribbean before. In that case, you may have difficulties understanding the patois, or more precisely, the Creole language, spoken by the people, which is based on the English language but sounds nothing like it to the untrained ear.

The Creole language is a blend of English, French, African, and other influences and has its own syntax, vocabulary, and pronunciation. For example, you may hear expressions like "wah gwan" (what's going on), "mek we go" (let's go), or "likkle more" (see you later). The Creole language is not written down or taught in schools, but it is a vital element of the culture and identity of St. Kitts and Nevis. You can learn some basic terms and phrases from friendly locals or internet resources, but don't worry if you can't comprehend everything - most people will revert to ordinary English when talking to strangers.

Climate

St. Kitts and Nevis has a tropical climate moderated by regular sea breezes. The average temperature varies from 24°C (75°F) to 30°C (86°F) throughout the year, with minimal seasonal change. The islands have lots of sunlight and clear skies, but they also endure infrequent rains and thunderstorms that maintain lush and green vegetation. The rainy season stretches from May through November, with September and October being the wettest months. The dry season stretches from December to April, with February and March being the driest months. The hurricane season overlaps with the rainy season; however, St. Kitts and Nevis is seldom impacted by big hurricanes. However, checking the weather prediction before your travel and taking measures if required is essential.

St. Kitts and Nevis is a place that provides a lot of fun and adventure for those who are searching for a distinctive Caribbean experience. By learning some basic facts about the island federation's currency, language, and climate, you can prepare yourself for a seamless and delightful journey that will leave you with lasting memories.

The emergency lines and health services

Traveling to St. Kitts and Nevis may be a fun and safe experience. However, you should be prepared for any emergency and know how to seek the necessary aid and support. Here are some valuable tips and information about the health services and emergency numbers of St. Kitts and Nevis, as well as some advice on how to keep healthy and prevent common health concerns.

Emergency Numbers

The emergency number for police, fire, and ambulance services in St. Kitts and Nevis is 911. Additional numbers are available for specific services.

- Hospital: 465-2551
- Police: 465-2241
- Coast Guard: 465-8384 / 466-9280
- Fire Department: 465-2515 / 465-7167
- Met Office: 465-2749

- Red Cross: 465-2584
- National Emergency Management Agency (NEMA): 466-5100
- COVID-19 Hotline: 765-4880 / 765-4095

It is essential to have these numbers stored on your phone or written down someplace accessible in case of an emergency. You should also have the contact information of your embassy or consulate in St. Kitts and Nevis and your travel insurance provider.

Health Services

St. Kitts and Nevis have a public health system offering citizens and residents free or subsidized health care. However, tourists are forced to pay for health treatments at public facilities unless they have a valid health insurance card from their home country or a reciprocal arrangement with St. Kitts and Nevis. Therefore, it is strongly advisable to have comprehensive travel insurance that covers medical expenditures, evacuation, and repatriation.

St. Kitts and Nevis have four public hospitals; three are in St. Kitts, and one is in Nevis. The biggest and best-equipped hospital is the Joseph N. France General Hospital in Basseterre, the capital of St. Kitts. The hospital features an emergency department, an intensive care unit, a maternity ward, a surgical unit, a laboratory, a pharmacy, and a radiology department. The hospital also features a helipad for air ambulance services.

The other public hospitals include the Mary Charles Hospital in Molineux, the Pogson Hospital in Sandy Point, and the Alexandra Hospital in Charlestown. These hospitals offer basic health care services, such as general medicine, pediatrics, obstetrics and gynecology, dentistry, and minor surgery. However, they may not have all the facilities and expertise that are accessible at the Joseph N. France General Hospital.

In addition to the public hospitals, there are an additional 17 health clinics dispersed over the two islands. These clinics provide basic health care services, such as vaccination, family planning, prenatal care, chronic illness management, mental health care, and HIV/AIDS testing and treatment. The clinics are open Monday through Friday from 8 a.m. to 4 p.m., except on public holidays.

St. Kitts and Nevis do not have any private hospitals, although many private doctors' clinics provide different healthcare services. Some of the private clinics are:

Caribbean Health Care Partners Ltd: This clinic provides general medicine, cardiology, dermatology, gastrointestinal, neurology, ophthalmology, orthopedics, urology, physiotherapy, radiography, laboratory testing, and pharmacy services.

Windsor University Health Center: This clinic includes general medical, pediatrics, psychiatry, psychology, dentistry, ophthalmology, physiotherapy, radiography, laboratory testing, and pharmacy services.

Ross University Health Center: This clinic includes general medicine, pediatrics, gynecology, psychiatry, psychology, dentistry, ophthalmology, physiotherapy, radiography, laboratory testing, and pharmacy services.

St. Kitts Biomedical Research Foundation: This clinic provides general medicine, cardiology, endocrinology, nephrology, rheumatology, allergy & immunology, dermatology, hematology, oncology, infectious diseases, genetics, and pharmacy services.

The private clinics charge fees for their services, which may vary based on the nature and complexity of the treatment. You should verify with your travel insurance carrier whether they cover the price of private health treatment in St. Kitts and Nevis.

St. Kitts and Nevis have a well-stocked supply of medicines and medical supplies because of their membership in the Eastern Caribbean Drug Service (ECDS), a regional pooled procurement program for importing pharmaceuticals and medical supplies. The ECDS helps the nation optimize the value of health care services to its inhabitants via the benefit of collective bulk procurement together with adjacent countries. The country's medicines business is mostly uncontrolled, with the exception of harmful medications. You can locate pharmacies in public hospitals and some private clinics, as well as select supermarkets and convenience shops. However, you should always see a doctor before taking any drug and carry a prescription for any medication you require or use frequently.

Health Tips

St. Kitts and Nevis are usually safe and healthy locations for tourists, but you should be aware of certain health concerns and problems and take measures against them. Here are some health suggestions to help you remain well and enjoy your trip:

Vaccination: You should be up to date with your usual immunizations, such as measles, mumps, rubella, diphtheria, tetanus, pertussis, polio, and influenza, before coming to St. Kitts and Nevis. You may also require certain more vaccines, such as hepatitis A, hepatitis B, typhoid, yellow fever, and rabies, depending on your trip plans and activity. You should contact your doctor or a travel health center at least four to six weeks before your trip to acquire the appropriate immunizations and guidance.

COVID-19: St. Kitts and Nevis have been afflicted by the COVID-19 pandemic, which has caused substantial delays to travel and health services. Before your trip, you should check the current travel warnings and entry criteria for St. Kitts and Nevis since they may change often depending on the circumstances. You should also observe the local health protocols and rules throughout your stay, such as wearing a mask, adopting social distancing, washing your hands often, and avoiding big gatherings. You should also monitor your health and get medical assistance if you experience any signs of COVID-19, such as fever, cough, shortness of breath, loss of taste or smell, or exhaustion. You should contact the COVID-19 hotline at 765-4880 or 765-4095 if you need any support or information about COVID-19 in St. Kitts & Nevis.

Mosquito-borne illnesses: St. Kitts and Nevis are in danger of mosquito-borne diseases, such as dengue fever, chikungunya, and Zika virus. These disorders may produce symptoms such as fever, headache, joint discomfort, rash, and nausea and can have significant implications in certain situations. There is no vaccination or specialized therapy for these illnesses. Thus, prevention is the best method. You should protect yourself against mosquito bites by applying insect repellent, wearing long-sleeved shirts and trousers, and sleeping beneath a mosquito net or in an air-conditioned room. You should also avoid stagnant water where mosquitoes grow and get medical assistance if you acquire any signs of mosquito-borne infections.

Food and water safety: St. Kitts and Nevis have a high quality of food and water safety, but you should still care while eating and drinking to prevent stomach disorders. You should only consume bottled or heated water and avoid ice cubes, tap water, and unpasteurized milk. You should also wash your hands before eating and avoid raw or undercooked food, particularly meat, shellfish, eggs, and dairy products. You should also peel or wash fruits and vegetables before consuming them and avoid food from street sellers or unsanitary settings. Suppose you have any symptoms of food poisoning, such as diarrhea, vomiting, stomach discomfort, or fever. In that case, you should drink lots of fluids to avoid dehydration and seek medical assistance if the symptoms are severe or persistent.

Sun exposure: St. Kitts and Nevis enjoy a tropical environment with high temperatures and humidity throughout the year. You should protect yourself from sun exposure to prevent sunburn, heatstroke, dehydration, and skin cancer. You should use sunscreen with a high SPF level, a hat, sunglasses, and light-colored clothes while outside. You should also drink enough water to keep hydrated and avoid alcohol and caffeine that might dehydrate you. You should also seek shade or air-conditioning during the warmest hours of the day and avoid vigorous activity in the heat. Suppose you feel any symptoms of sun exposure, such as redness, blistering, headache, dizziness, nausea, or disorientation. In that case, you should cool down using cold compresses or showers, drink drinks to rehydrate yourself, and seek medical treatment if the symptoms worsen.

Summary

If you go to St. Kitts and Nevis, you may anticipate a nice and safe vacation. However, if you experience any emergency circumstance, you should know how to receive aid and support. The number to contact for any emergency service, such as police, fire, or ambulance, is 911.

The important websites and apps for travelers

If you visit St. Kitts and Nevis, you will want to know more about these magnificent Caribbean islands and their offerings. You may discover useful and accurate information and assistance from numerous websites and applications that cater to tourists who wish to experience the finest of St. Kitts and Nevis. Here are some websites and applications you may use and access during your journey to these islands.

Websites

St. Kitts Tourism

St. Kitts Tourism is the official website of the St. Kitts Tourism Authority, which promotes and develops tourism on the island of St. Kitts. It offers valuable data, news, events, and resources for tourists who desire to visit St. Kitts. You may also get information about the island's history, culture, nature, attractions, activities, lodgings, transportation, and more. You may also obtain a free brochure or sign up for a newsletter to remain informed on the latest activities in St. Kitts. You may reach St. Kitts Tourism's website at stkittstourism.kn.

Website: stkittstourism.kn

Apps

SKNIS

SKNIS stands for St. Kitts and Nevis Information Service, the official news agency of the government of St. Kitts and Nevis. It delivers timely and reliable news and information on the events of the government and the country. You may download the SKNIS app on your smartphone or tablet to access news articles, press releases, audio clips, videos, photographs, and social media feeds from SKNIS. You may also listen to live broadcasts from ZIZ Radio or watch live broadcasts from ZIZ TV on the app. The SKNIS app is available for free on both iOS and Android smartphones.

App name: SKNIS Download link: [iOS] | [Android]

Nevis Naturally

Nevis Naturally is the official app of the Nevis Tourism Authority, which promotes and develops tourism on the island of Nevis. It thoroughly references Nevis, providing information on the island's history, culture, environment, attractions, activities, lodgings, food choices, transportation, and more. You may also get maps, photographs, videos, reviews, events, bargains, and advice on the app. Call the Nevis Tourism Authority or book your vacation online using the app. The Nevis Naturally app is free for iOS and Android smartphones.

App name: Nevis Naturally Download link: [iOS] | [Android]

Custom and Etiquette

Greetings and Introductions

The most typical method to welcome someone in St. Kitts and Nevis is to say "Good morning," "Good afternoon," or "Good evening," depending on the time of day. You may also say "Hello" or "Hi," although they are less formal and more informal. When approaching someone for the first time, it is courteous to shake hands and introduce yourself with your name and where you are from. If you meet someone of the opposite gender, you may also add praise, such as "You look lovely today" or "You have a nice smile." However, avoid getting overly intimate or provocative since this may be regarded as unpleasant or insulting.

When welcoming someone you already know, you may additionally embrace or kiss them on the cheek, depending on your familiarity and friendliness. However, this is more frequent among women than men, who generally just embrace or kiss their close relatives or acquaintances. If you are unsure how to welcome someone, following their example and duplicating their gesture is advisable.

When addressing someone in St. Kitts and Nevis, it is courteous to use their title and surname, such as "Mr. Jones" or "Mrs. Smith," unless they allow you to use their personal name. You may also say "Sir" or "Ma'am" if you do not know their name or title. However, avoid using nicknames or words of affection, such as "Honey" or "Sweetie," unless you are close to the individual.

Conversation and Communication The official language of St. Kitts and Nevis is English, although many inhabitants also speak a Creole dialect influenced by African, French, Spanish, and Dutch languages. You may hear certain words or phrases that are unknown to you, such as "wah gwan" (what's going on), "irie" (all right), or "liming" (hanging around). You might ask the speaker to clarify what they mean or repeat what they said if you do not understand them. However, avoid ridiculing or copying their accent or dialect since this may be perceived as disrespectful or condescending.

The inhabitants of St. Kitts and Nevis are typically pleasant, extroverted, and chatty and like having talks with guests. They are fascinated by your past, ideas, and experiences and will ask you numerous questions about yourself and your nation. You may answer questions honestly and freely, but avoid bragging or boasting about your income, position, or accomplishments since this may be considered arrogant or impolite. You may also ask them questions about their culture, history, and lifestyle, but avoid sensitive or controversial themes, such as politics, religion, and racism.

The inhabitants of St. Kitts and Nevis are very expressive and lively in their Communication and utilize gestures, facial expressions, and body language to communicate their emotions and attitudes. You may observe that they nod their head to indicate no or down to express yes or point with their lips or chin instead of their fingers. You may attempt to analyze their non-verbal signs and react appropriately, but avoid duplicating or imitating them since this may be perceived as mocking or insulting.

The inhabitants of St. Kitts and Nevis are also witty and lighthearted in their Communication and prefer to joke and tease one another and with guests. You may hear someone utilize sarcasm, irony, or exaggeration to convey a point or to make fun of a situation or a person. You may engage in the banter and laugh along with them, but avoid offending or becoming upset since this may be perceived as overreacting or overly sensitive. You may also make jokes or tease them back, but avoid personal or sensitive issues, such as their looks, family, or culture.

Dress and Appearance The dress code in St. Kitts and Nevis is usually casual and informal, particularly on the beaches and in the resorts. You may wear light and comfortable apparel, such as shorts, t-shirts, sandals, and sunglasses, to deal with the tropical temperature and the laid-back environment. However, you should also carry some formal and conservative apparel, such as long trousers, skirts, dresses, shirts, and shoes, for events that need greater respect and decorum, such as visiting churches, government offices, or fancy restaurants. You should also avoid wearing camouflage clothes or accessories since this is forbidden in St. Kitts and Nevis.

Regarding looks, the people of St. Kitts and Nevis are proud of their ancestry and identity and prefer to express themselves via their hair, jewelry, tattoos, and piercings. Some persons may wear dreadlocks, braids, beads, rings, or other adornments representing their culture and individuality. You should accept their decisions and preferences and avoid looking at or remarking on their looks. You should also avoid touching or playing with their hair or accessories without their consent since this may be perceived as invasive or impolite.

Gifts and Invitations The inhabitants of St. Kitts and Nevis are kind and friendly and may welcome you to their homes or activities throughout your visit. If you get an invitation, you should accept it if feasible since this is a gesture of friendship and confidence. You should also bring a modest present for your host or hostess, such as a bottle of wine, a box of chocolates, or a souvenir from your country. You should also volunteer to assist with preparing or cleaning the meal or celebration since this is regarded as polite and respectful.

When you arrive at your host's house or function, you should greet everyone with a handshake and a smile. You should also wait for your host to show you where to sit or what to do. You should follow their example and obey their customs and traditions. For example, you may be requested to join in a prayer or a toast before eating or drinking or to engage in a game or a dance after the meal or the celebration. You should strive to be courteous and enthusiastic and avoid dismissing or refusing their offers since this may be considered disrespectful or ungrateful.

When you leave your host's house or event, thank them for their hospitality and kindness and congratulate them on their cuisine, décor, or entertainment. You should also say farewell to everyone present and wish them well. You may also send a thank-you card or a message to your host the following day, expressing your thanks and thankfulness.

CONCLUSION

St. Kitts and Nevis is a place that provides something for everyone. Whether searching for a calm beach holiday, a cultural immersion, or an adventure-filled escape, you will find it in this tropical paradise. You may explore the historical and cultural attractions of Basseterre and Charlestown, discover the natural beauty of the rainforest and the volcano, enjoy the beach and the sea activities, or indulge in the gastronomic pleasures and the nightlife. You may also enjoy the difference and complementarity of the two islands, each with its charm and individuality.

Getting to and around St. Kitts and Nevis is easy and uncomplicated. You can fly to St. Kitts from several significant cities in Europe and North America or take a boat from adjacent islands like St. Maarten or Antigua. You may also go by boat between St. Kitts and Nevis, which is a short and economical excursion of 45 minutes and $10. Based on your budget and comfort, you may select your favorite form of transportation on the islands, such as a vehicle, bike, bus, or taxi.

The people of St. Kitts and Nevis are warm and welcoming, and they will make you feel like you belong. You will also encounter a rich and varied culture that exhibits the island's history and legacy. You will listen to English with a Caribbean accent and also Creole languages such as Nevisian or Patois. You will see festivals and activities that are vibrant and that celebrate the island's cultures and traditions. You will relish exquisite cuisine that blends African, European, Indian, and Amerindian influences.

St. Kitts and Nevis is a place that will leave you with amazing recollections of your journey. You will have fun, study, rest, and enjoy every second of your visit. You will also love the island's beauty, charm, and character. You will want to come back again and again.

Made in the USA
Las Vegas, NV
20 October 2023

79444341R00125